Trust is Everything

Become the Leader Others Will Follow

Aneil K. Mishra

Karen E. Mishra

ISBN: 978-0-6151-9910-8

Library of Congress Control Number: 2008904512

Dedicated to

Maggie Chandra and Jack Chandra
Who illuminate us each and every day

Acknowledgments

There are many people along the way who have been helpful and supportive as we wrote this book. We would first like to thank the leaders profiled in this book who inspired us to tell their stories. We are grateful to them for generously sharing their time with us. We also want to thank the many employees who shared their valuable insights about their leaders.

We are also grateful to the many people who over the years helped us refine our thinking about trust and gave us valuable feedback as well. Aneil's dissertation committee members were instrumental in helping him develop the framework of trust: Professors Kim Cameron, Dan Denison, Jane Dutton, Rick Bagozzi, and Marvin Peterson. Bridgette Briggs Trujillo served as Aneil's research assistant when he was a doctoral student, and helped him identify some of the key elements of trust in his interview data. We also have had several colleagues who have provided us with important feedback as we conducted our research and wrote the book: Professors Denise Rousseau, Gretchen Spreitzer, and David Lassman; authors Jackie Huba and Dr. John Gordon; and Aneil's assistant at Wake Forest University, Lynn Ebert. Finally, we thank our countless undergraduate and MBA students as well as executive education participants, who helped us refine our thoughts as we went about the development and writing of this book.

Contents

I

The ROCC of Trust

1

Leaders are Born and Made

It is an equal failing to trust everybody, and to trust nobody. - English Proverb

This is the universal question: Are leaders born or made? We have tried to teach our students and clients over the years that leaders are born *and* made. By this we mean that even though some individuals are naturally more inclined to become leaders, based on their early life experiences and yes, even genetics, all people have the capacity to become leaders if they have the desire and make the effort to do so. Some people are more empathetic than others, some are more energetic, and some are more engaging than others. Each person has a unique composition of talents, motives, and dreams that provide the raw material for getting the best out of everyone around them. Everyone can draw upon something in their background and experiences to become more effective at leading others if they really want to.

We base our teachings on the opportunities we have had to work with leaders who consistently keep their commitments, are frank almost to a fault, perform incredibly, while seeking to better the lives of those around them rather than simply filling their own bank accounts. These people act both humbly and heroically, but are not superhuman or unbelievable. They may be extraordinary leaders, but they are still ordinary people that rose to the challenge of creating transformational change by building what we call *The ROCC of Trust.* The ROCC of Trust stands for the four key types of trustworthiness that we have found to be the key elements that influence people to trust in a leader: Reliability, Openness, Competence, and Compassion. We believe that by profiling these leaders' and telling their stories, they can inspire and guide us so that we, too, can develop and sustain the ROCC of Trust with those around us.

Why We Wrote This Book

We wrote this book because trust was rare in the contexts we had worked in and studied. We both worked for General Motors in the 1980s when it was going through a significant upheaval with threats from Japanese competition, lack of trust with respect to their customers, and significant downsizing. In this situation, we found only one manager that we trusted and respected enough to want to continue to work at GM. We then went on to graduate school where studied the automotive industry during a period of downsizing. We conducted interviews with scores of leaders and managers in the automotive industry, and once again found only one leader who had built trust with his employees, customers, and suppliers. He turned around a plant that was going to be shut because of its horrible costs, quality and productivity, and transformed it into GM's best plant in North America, saving thousands of employee's jobs and generating hundreds of millions of dollars in bottom line improvements to the company. The example of this man, Bob Lintz, convinced us that trust was a very powerful force for positive change, that ordinary people could build it, but that it was not easy to do.

As we found other ordinary people who became extraordinary leaders by building trust, we wanted to share these examples because they demonstrate that trust is not just some elusive, squishy concept, but a of thinking, feeling, and acting that can contribute significant improvements to the bottom line of an organization. Our scholarly research shows that trust can be measured systematically, improved through key practices, and that it enhances employee commitment; reduces unwanted employee turnover; and improves business unit productivity, innovation, and efficiency. These kinds of performance results are especially important for today's organizations to be competitive.

People Don't Trust Their Leaders

Do you totally trust the leaders of the organizations you belong to and work in? If you are like the people we have studied over the past two decades, then you probably don't. National polls regularly document the lack of trust we have in our political, business, and social organizations (see for example the annual trust survey at www.edelman.com).

This is a horrible state of affairs. Why do people trust their colleagues more than their leaders? The inept or dishonest leaders of such firms as AIG, Fannie Mae and Freddie Mac, Merrill Lynch, Tyco, Enron, Long-Term Capital Management, and Société Générale, to name just a few, are partly to blame of course. This is also probably because many private and public sector leaders, despite their rhetoric, have not made the necessary effort to build trust with their key stakeholders, including their employees, their customers or suppliers, or their communities.

Nevertheless, we have identified some compelling examples of trustworthy leaders from a wide variety of organizations, both for-profit and not-for-profit operating in a wide variety of circumstances. Our findings are based on a long-term research program investigating the role of trust and organizational effectiveness in a wide variety of circumstances. As part of this ongoing research program, we have surveyed thousands of managers and employees representing scores of firms in both the manufacturing and service sectors, and interviewed over a hundred executives and employees at different levels of responsibility in a wide variety of industries. We have also examined the relationship among trust, employee commitment, and employee turnover in both a multibillion dollar firm and a much smaller firm over a period of several years (see Appendix B for a list of our published research articles).

The ROCC of Trust

Simply put, trusting others means you are willing to be vulnerable to them in the face of uncertainty. If we trust someone, we are more willing to become interdependent with that person, even though we can't be absolutely sure everything will turn out fine. The benefits we have discovered from building trust include deeper, more loyal relationships, stronger resiliency in the face of a crisis, and enhanced individual, team and organizational performance. Over the past two decades, through our research, teaching, coaching, and consulting work, we have identified four basic ways in which individuals trust their leaders and one another: **R**eliability, **O**penness, **C**ompetence, and **C**ompassion, which we call **the ROCC of Trust**. The ROCC of Trust does *not* mean blind faith. When individuals have the ROCC of Trust in their leader, it is based on repeated experiences that have been validated in a variety of situations. When a leader has developed The ROCC of Trust, it means that he or she has earned the privilege to be depended upon when events go well and when they do not.

Reliability

The ROCC of Trust starts with Reliability. When someone can rely on us, we behave in a way that is even and consistent. We are dependable. We do something when we say we will and we show up when we say we will. We remember things that are important to that person and we become a source of stability in their life. Reliability is the first piece of the ROCC of Trust – without it, others will not give us a second chance.

Openness

Openness is a willingness to be honest and forthright in your dealings with others. If others believe we are honest, they will trust what we have to say to them. Our openness also encourages more openness from others. If we are honest with our neighbor, co-worker or family member, they become more willing to open up to us. This mutual exchange of information creates a more trusting relationship. Being open also includes being fair and evenhanded in sharing information or perspectives. It is the second piece of the ROCC of Trust.

Competence

Competence is the third piece of the ROCC of Trust. Even if we are viewed as reliable and honest, people will not want to trust us unless we can do the job. There are times that we use proxies for competence, such as a specific degree from a certain college, but direct experience with another person is a more convincing way to demonstrate competence. It is perhaps the easiest of the pieces of the ROCC of Trust to improve upon. If we are not as competent as we would like to be in a certain area, we can always improve upon the abilities we have.

Compassion

Compassion is the last piece of the ROCC of Trust. Having compassion for others means that we must be willing to set aside our own self-concern in order to be truly empathetic of others. It also means that we must put the interests of others at a level equal to or above our own. This is the last aspect of trust we find in others, because the others are easier to come by. Being a truly compassionate person takes an investment of time and requires us to demonstrate empathy. That is why compassion is valued so highly.

The ROCC of Trust

The four pieces or dimensions of trust, Reliability, Openness, Competence and Compassion together form the ROCC of Trust: a solid foundation on which we can put our faith in others. When all four of those pieces are in place, we have *The ROCC of Trust* in another person. In contrast, when even one of the pieces of the ROCC is missing, we may not want to make ourselves vulnerable to that individual. Obviously, certain pieces of the ROCC are more important in certain contexts than in others. When we deal with physicians, we probably care more about their compassion than when we deal with our dry cleaners. Even the same piece of the ROCC matters more depending on the person we are trusting. Competence matters both when dealing with physicians and dry cleaners, but our vulnerability is greater when someone has the power to make us healthier or sicker than when the person can either clean our clothes properly or shrink them.

Trust Tips

The concept of trust is central to who we do business with and why. Our perception of trust enables us to distinguish between someone we would hire to work on our team and someone we would decline to hire. Zig Ziglar reminds us that "People buy from people they trust."

With trust being so important, we need to focus energy every single day in making sure that our colleagues, customers, and suppliers all believe that we are worthy of their trust. We must also be able to find ways to trust them.

These Trust Tips highlight the four aspects of Trust we have found in our research, consulting, coaching and teaching that help us become more trustworthy and more trusting. We call it the **ROCC of Trust.**

Organization of This Book

Our journey has several parts. We first begin by identifying several characteristics that bind together the leaders who demonstrate The ROCC of Trust: courage, authenticity, and humility. Together these leadership attributes encourage people to be vulnerable to their leaders and to one another, which is essential if leaders are to achieve their goals. We then define what The ROCC of Trust is, and discuss how leaders who are courageous, authentic, and humble are able to build and sustain such trust in a wide variety of organizations and circumstances. Our journey then continues by showing how leaders sustain or reestablish the ROCC of Trust they've built, even in the face of long-standing conflicts, widespread complacency, or during crisis. Finally, we "complete" our journey by showing how our leaders have been able to rebuild trust once it has been lost or broken, one of the hardest tasks anyone has to do, and one that is rarely accomplished.

Trust Tips Dos and Don'ts

Do:

- Do determine who you trust and who you don't and why.
- Do identify who trusts you and who doesn't and why.
- Do realize how important your trusted friends are.
- Do demonstrate genuine compassion for others' needs and concerns.

Don't:

- Don't make excuses for the times when you aren't dependable.
- Don't ever fail to tell the truth, even when you can get away with a lie.
- Don't be shy about asking for help if you need it to improve your performance.
- Don't forget to make the time to help others who need your time and energy.

The next chapter describes how great leaders build trust, by being courageous, by being authentic, and by showing humility.

2

The Three Pillars of Trust

Example is not the main thing in influencing others—it's the only thing. - Albert Schweitzer (Maxwell, p. 76)

ROCC Stars have Courage, Authenticity and Humility

We found three characteristics in common among the leaders we have worked with who have demonstrated The ROCC of Trust: courage, authenticity, and humility. We call these people our "ROCC Stars." Their courage allowed them to be vulnerable to others, which is critical in starting to build trust. Their authenticity encouraged others in turn to be vulnerable to them. Finally, the leaders' humility fostered their followers and others to be vulnerable to each other.

Courage

Mary Ellen Sheets told us that she started her company, Two Men and a Truck (TMT), when she found out her bosses at the State of Michigan kept refusing to promote her and assuming she'd never leave. Her sons had been moving others' goods and furniture as a way to earn money for college during their summers. When her sons returned to college, the phone kept ringing, and Mary Ellen decided to hire two guys, named Joe and Elmer (literally) and purchased a used truck to keep this side business going and supplement her income as a data analyst for the State of Michigan. Without any formal training, she did the bookkeeping, scheduling, customer relations, fleet management, hiring, and firing. The actual moving she delegated to Joe and Elmer. Eventually, she left the comfort of her government job to run the business as a full-time career. From a $350 initial investment in the truck, her franchise-based firm now grosses more than $200 million annually.

Humility

Bob Lintz was just a college-graduate in training when he initially was hired by General Motors. Soon after he was on the job, the general superintendent came to welcome him to the plant. He said "welcome, Robert," and asked him what he could to help him. Bob said that only his parents ever called him Robert, and the only thing he would like would be to be called "Bob." The general superintendent answered him, "yes, Robert." Bob vowed that from that day on, he would insist that his subordinates call him Bob. Bob eliminated other barriers between management and labor by not wearing a tie and eliminating the executive dining room.

By removing these and other barriers, Bob was able to transform the $250 million Parma, Ohio stamping plant scheduled to be shut down in three years into a billion dollar enterprise that has lasted more than 20 years after it was supposed be closed. For this long-term success to have been achieved, it had to begin with the way that Bob dealt with everyone, including his own management team:

We had meeting agendas for my management team, and I couldn't wait to talk because I've got a lot of energy and I want to sell my points. I know times when I went into those meetings and seven items are on there and I come of the meeting 0 for 7. I wasn't even close to having the best quality decision. I walked out of there a lot of times thinking, 'Why did I even open my mouth? I would walk out of my office with my head down thinking, 'oh, they must think I'm a complete idiot. Then, to recapture my self-esteem, I would say to myself, 'The good thing is that I helped create an environment where we can talk like that, we can make decisions like that, because they're going to be impacting thousands of people in the community, and the best quality decisions were made.'

Authenticity

Ted Castle coached collegiate hockey for the University of Vermont and had a small family ice cream business on the side. His company, Rhino Foods, adheres to the philosophy that life is a game to be won by playing fairly and honestly. "We try to bring a lot of what motivates people in a game, any kind of game, into our business." He realized that his employees would be more motivated if they knew the rules, were told the score, and could succeed by hard work.

In order to encourage his employees to think more like owners, even though his firm was and is privately owned, Ted opened his books to show his employees how to make the firm more profitable. Then, if his employees improved earnings, they received a share of the profits. This built a great deal of trust with his employees because he was being open about sharing sensitive financial information, as well as demonstrating compassion for their well-being by sharing his company' success. Rhino Foods worked with Ben & Jerry's to develop its *Cookie Dough Ice Cream*, helping Ben & Jerry's to be the first company to create such an ice cream product. Rhino Foods still supplies Ben & Jerry's with the cookie dough that goes into their ice cream. Rhino Foods now grosses more than $30 million annually.

Getting Real Builds Trust

Bob Lintz was once invited to the wedding of one of the children of the local United Auto Worker (UAW) union leader while he was plant manager. Bob said that this would have been unheard of under the previous management of his plant. All of Mary Ellen's employees and franchisees know her well enough to call her by her first name. She is humble also in acknowledging that she has made mistakes in leading her company. Her goal, however, is to help franchisees be the most profitable that they can be. By serving her franchisees this way, she and the firm are able to expect that the franchisees will be similarly motivated to serve their customers. When business circumstances turned tough, a servant leaders like Rhino Foods' Ted Castle was able to ask his best employees to go to work for a different local firm doing seasonal work. They believed his promise that their jobs would be given back once the market picked up. The firms who were able to borrow Ted's employees in turn provided Rhino Foods with the flexibility essential to dealing with a volatile business environment, and they want to do so again in the future.

In other words, these leaders' courage, authenticity, and humility created very strong trust with their employees, customers, suppliers, and communities. Without their courage, the distrust that is typical in their industries would have been impossible to overcome. Because of their authenticity, employees believed that they could succeed together with their leaders. Their humility fostered sustainable growth and allowed them to overcome significant obstacles. These "ROCC Stars" created virtuous cycles of trust by viewing others as either friends or people waiting to be befriended. These virtual trust cycles encouraged individuals and groups to provide the flexibility, initiative, and sacrifices essential not only to survival during tough times, but also to lasting success.

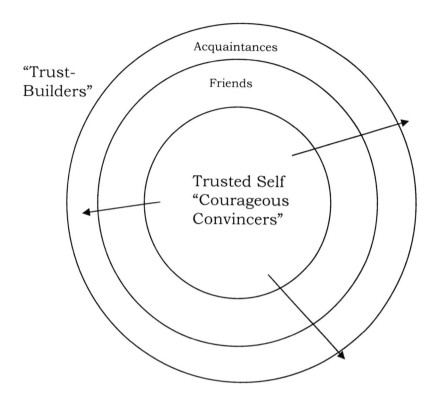

Getting Lost Prevents Trust

In contrast, without courage, leaders aren't willing to find out how others view them. They lack self-awareness, and so they can't be authentic. They aren't humble, and so they aren't open to negative feedback. They view everyone as outsiders, competitors, or outright enemies. Not surprisingly, those around in turn distrust them. Such leaders are truly lost, or soon become lost, unable to work with others to overcome uncertainties, resolve conflicts, or expand their influence. Vicious cycles ensue in which lack of cooperation, cynicism, and suspicion beget more counterproductive behavior which validates the initial distrust.

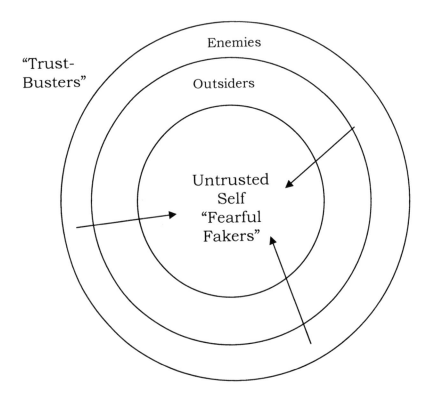

Trust Tips Dos and Don'ts

Do:

- Do act courageously enough to admit your mistakes
- Do be humble enough to ask others for help.
- Do encourage others to share their opinions.

Don't:

- Don't be arrogant and assume you have all the answers.
- Don't be what you think others want you to be – be yourself.
- Don't shut out negative feedback.

The next chapter describes the first piece of the ROCC of Trust – Reliability.

3

Reliability: The First Piece of the ROCC of Trust

I do not believe in contrived ways of building trust. If one just talks the talk and walks the walk, and makes their own behavior consistent with the objectives and values of the organization, then folks will trust you. If you are a hypocrite, they will soon find that out as well....Do what you say you're going to do when you say you're going to do it. - Dennis Quaintance, Quaintance-Weaver Enterprises

Reliability is the first piece of the ROCC of Trust because it is typically the first aspect we notice with respect to another person's trustworthiness. At a minimum, it means doing what you say you're going to do. It also means keeping one's promises and "walking the talk." It can be as simple as showing up on time for an appointment, and as difficult as keeping commitments in times of significant adversity.

Reliability, then, is the first way that we can demonstrate to other people that we are trustworthy. Before they know if we are compassionate, open or even competent, they can test to see if we are reliable—do we keep our promises, do we "do" what we say we will do, do we follow-through? We might even ask in what way we are reliable. We all have different talents and abilities. The key is to find something that you are good at and something that you enjoy being reliable at and then do it. There are many ways to be reliable, such as getting to work on time, generating reports in a timely manner, working late when needed, and even remembering to send birthday cards.

Act Tough but Don't be a Tyrant

By the beginning of 1994, even though TMT (www.twomen.com) had grown to 35 franchisees and $6.7 million in annual revenues and almost double the amount a year earlier, Mary Ellen was still doing everything herself—the newsletter, the annual meeting, visiting franchises, and the accounting. She knew the franchisees so well that she not only knew the names of their children, but the year and make of each of their moving trucks. In addition, Mary Ellen was successfully running her own franchise in Lansing, which was growing very quickly, allowing her to quit her job with the State of Michigan.

At the same time the company was experiencing such tremendous growth (at the end of 1994, revenues would exceed $10 million), Mary Ellen was asked by the Michigan Republican Party to run for state Senate. She knew that she would need assistance and asked her daughter, Melanie, to step in as president and run the day-to-day operations of the company, and her son, Jon, to run her franchise in Lansing. Melanie agreed to take on the job of president even though the job paid no salary, and even though it meant giving up an $80,000 a year job with a company car. She did so because she realized that her mom really needed help, and not just because Mary Ellen was going to run for political office.

Melanie brought to the company her experience as a pharmaceutical sales representative, as well as her experience running franchises in Georgia and Michigan. Right way, Melanie saw the need to introduce formal controls into the franchise system. Because Mary Ellen had personally brought in every franchisee and wanted to help them grow their business, she was lax about allowing the franchisees to make royalty payments on time. Melanie felt very strongly that she needed to apply the franchise agreement fairly across all franchisees in order to protect the value of the TMT brand. In addition to those franchises that had been tardy in their royalty payments, several of the franchises decided to stop paying royalties altogether.

Some of the franchisees who had "grown up" with Mary Ellen wondered what this young woman Melanie was really made of, and decided to put her to the test. In response to Melanie enforcing the franchise agreements more consistently and raising the royalty rate, six of the more disgruntled franchisees banded together, taking advantage of some loopholes in the franchise agreement, and threatened to use the TMT name and logo but not pay royalties due to TMT International. Melanie invested significant sums of her own money to cover the mounting legal bills and to fight the six delinquent franchises in court in order to make sure that TMT's franchise agreement was upheld. She took the lead in TMT's legal battle against the rogue franchises, even though she also was raising twin six-month old boys at the time, and her husband was fighting a battle with cancer. Melanie noted that the legal costs were in excess of $600,000, and that at one point "we were so broke we just kept the heat turned down really low. We were freezing in that house just to cut down on expenses. We had to start telling our vendors that we couldn't pay them in full, including our attorneys. We sent our attorneys $500 a month, even though we owed them several hundred thousand dollars."

The court, however, eventually upheld the TMT franchise agreement. Two of the six franchisees apologized and asked if they could return to the system while the other four were terminated. As part of the settlement, TMT and its franchisees would not operate in the state of Georgia. Eventually, **TWO MEN AND A TRUCK**® bought the rights back for the state of Georgia and currently has 14 franchise locations operating in that state.

In addition to achieving the court settlement with the rogue franchises, she raised the royalty rate from 4% to 6% for all franchises. Melanie personally visited every one of the franchisees to explain the rationale for the rate increase. This also allowed her to meet each franchisee so that could get to know her personally as she assumed many of her mom's duties. While the royalty rate TMT charges is within the range for the franchising in general (6-8%), the advertising fee that TMT charges, 1%, is much less than the industry average of 2-3%, according to Matt Cutler, Vice President of Franchise Development & Government

Relations. One likely reason for the lower rate is, of course, that positive word of mouth from TMT's customers means that Home Office doesn't need to spend a great deal of money on advertising its services.

As Mary Ellen herself said "I am probably the soft person and Melanie is the other person." Sally Degnan, former Training Director agrees. "Mary Ellen rules with her heart. Melanie has a heart, but rules with her mind." Such toughness, however, tempered by her zealousness for fairness, was absolutely critical to the long-term survival and success of TMT. Because of Melanie's insistence on fair and consistent dealings with respect to royalty payments, she proved to all of the franchisees in the TMT system that they could count on her. Without her diligence, it is likely that TMT would have failed as a company. Instead, it has continued to prosper and grow, and at the end of 2007, had exceeded more than $200 million in annual revenues. In 2008, it was named one of the nation's "25 High-Performing Franchises" by the *Wall Street Journal* in February, 2008.[1]

---

[1] Raymund Flandez, "A Look at High-Performing Franchises: Food's Grip Loosens As Diverse Concepts Pop Up and Do Well," *The Wall Street Journal*, February 13, 2008. http://online.wsj.com/article/SB120277576323060649.html?mod=Franchising

Trust Tips Dos and Don'ts

Do:

- Do show up on time, all the time.
- Do make sure your deeds follow your words.
- Do let others know when circumstances change.

Don't:

- Don't create different standards for different stakeholders.
- Don't be arbitrary in enforcing your organization's policies.
- Don't make promises you can't keep.

In the next chapter, we describe the importance of Openness in the ROCC of Trust.

4

Openness: The Second Piece of the ROCC of Trust

If they don't believe what I'm telling them, if they think it's all a bunch of bull, don't expect them to go out there and work a little harder or work a little different. They're not going to be as receptive to change unless they understand and trust that the things that I'm talking about are in fact true. - Automotive executive

At a minimum, being open means not lying to another person. At its greatest level it means full disclosure. One form of such disclosure that the leaders we have worked with have demonstrated is their willingness to admit they don't know everything, which empowers their followers to help them out. Our definition of openness includes creating a climate of honest dialogue by disclosing information with each other in an effort to create a more trusting relationship. In this effort, motives, agendas, and goals become more transparent -- we tell it like it is— what you see is what you get. It is easy to demonstrate reliability first—there is little downside or risk in being reliable first; but there are real risks in being open first— there is the risk that your employees, partners, colleagues or customers might interpret the information you share with them in the wrong way, might take advantage of such information, or fail to reciprocate your openness.

Reliability can be demonstrated more quickly than Openness. You can prove that at your first meeting with someone. Openness takes longer to develop. Because there is a level of vulnerability to being open, we keep our guard up and develop a spirit of openness much more slowly. Think of how friendships are formed. You don't often make a best friend in a day—it often takes time to meet someone, get to know them, share experiences with them, share life stories with them, then really know them on a deeper level. It is even more challenging in a work environment. We have so many more walls developed around us to prevent us from being open with one another – walls between cubicles, departments, hierarchies, and even walls between customers and suppliers. All of these barriers prevent us from being open with each other until we feel that we have had sufficient time getting to know one another. Even then, we may not let that happen if we are not sufficiently secure in ourselves.

However, we have found that those leaders that have the courage to be open with their constituents are rewarded with greater levels of trust by their followers. That is how trust is built by openness in its essence -- your willingness to be vulnerable by sharing information in order for others to trust you.

Open Books, Open Minds

Nevertheless, there are still real risks in practicing openness. One risk is that they may interpret what you tell them in the wrong way. When Ted Castle, President of privately held Rhino Foods thought about opening his company's books to his employees he was concerned that if they only focused on sales without understanding expenses, cash flow, or the cost of capital among other aspects of a firm's bottom line, they would think the business was making tons of profits, when in fact most of it was simply revenue. Such information could also have been shared with Rhino Foods' competitors, leaving his firm at a competitive disadvantage. In 1990, he decided to proceed anyway and it was the right decision for his company because his employees began to take ownership for the profitability of the firm. But as we will read later, it was *how* he shared his financial information, and *how* employees were rewarded for using such information responsibly, that gave his employees a true sense of ownership.

Another risk is that demonstrating openness might not be reciprocated, leaving you at an informational disadvantage and potentially vulnerable as a result. For example, you might find yourself sharing information about your feelings with a colleague who then decides that they do not wish to share any information about how they feel. You might feel silly or ashamed that you were left "high and dry," as you thought they might share information with you, too.

Trust Tips Do's and Don'ts

Do:

- Do identify what people in your organization would like to know more about.
- Do schedule regular time to share information with your colleagues.
- Do take concrete steps to be more open and honest with others.

Don't:

- Don't be afraid to be the first person to share information.
- Don't forget to treat the information you receive back from others with as much care and
- respect as you expect they treat your information.

The following chapter explains how being competent is the next critical piece of the ROCC of Trust.

5

Competence: The Third Piece of the ROCC of Trust

Be a yardstick of quality. Some people aren't used to an environment where excellence is expected. - Stephen Jobs

Competence is a person's ability or skill level to perform a certain task. At a minimum, it means being able to perform ably and meet others' performance expectations. At its highest level, it means consistently exceeding such expectations. There are many proxies for competence, including one's prior track record and educational achievements. There are times that we engage a person to work for or with us before we really know for ourselves whether or not they can do the job we need them to do. When we ask someone new to be on the board of our non-profit organization, we might invite them based on the recommendation of a colleague at work or a friend at church. We probably have not served on a board with them in the past, but we trust our colleague or friend enough that we trust their judgment and invite that person onto our board.

Our research shows that competence takes longer than reliability to develop in the ROCC of Trust. It is possible for you to demonstrate your reliability before anyone knows for sure whether or not you are competent. Like Reliability, Competence is something, however, we can demonstrate fairly easily—either we can do the job, or we can't. When we do demonstrate competence, it makes others more willing to follow us because they believe that we can provide solutions to issues that are important to them.

From Bad Overtime to Good Overtime

In the case of Bob Lintz, he proclaimed from the beginning that he did not know how to run every piece of machinery in the Parma plant. What he did know how to do was to organize and motivate people to do their best on their piece of equipment so that the whole plant would function as competently as possible. Over time, he demonstrated his own competence and that of his plant and his employees as well.

When Bob assumed the position of Plant Manager at Parma, it had one of the worst labor relations climates within GM. It was a $250 million operation, which was expected to be shut down within three years. Even by 1990, when it was a $700 million operation, it had no expectation of long-term survival, given GM's continued declining market share and excess capacity in stamping operations, and Parma's poor inefficiency and labor productivity relative to its Japanese competitors. By 1998, however, even though revenues had only increased somewhat to $750 million, the Parma Plant was now producing at this level with one-third fewer employees (3175 versus 4700 in 1990). Quality had also improved dramatically, as Parma became a preferred supplier within GM and achieved QS 9000 certification. The productivity and quality improvements were so significant by 1998 that the Parma plant was able to eliminate $20 million in annual overtime, labeled "bad overtime" because it had been used out of the need to make up for low productivity or poor quality. This resulted in the average hourly employee losing $10,000 in annual wages, with some skilled tradespeople losing as much as $25,000 in annual pay. The only way they could recoup these earnings would be if Parma succeeded in acquiring new products to build from GM, resulting in additional work. Their trust in the leadership at Parma was such that they were willing to give up their "bad overtime" for the hope of "good overtime" in the future.

The next decade's improvements would prove to be even more dramatic. By 2004, Parma was rated GM's best stamping plant world-wide. It repeated this achievement in 2005, when Parma's revenues exceeded over $1 billion, and it was also the best stamping plant, Japanese or American, in North America. In 2007, eight years after Bob Lintz retired from GM, Parma is now one of the best, most efficient stamping plants in the world, including its Japanese competitors (*2007 Habour Report*). As Bob told us in October of 2007:

The plant today would absolutely knock your socks off. You would not believe it. You wouldn't be able to tell the difference between an hourly employee from a salaried employee either by looking at them or talking to them. You could talk to any person in that plant and he's going to know his job inside and out. Our hourly employees establish their own quality standards, and write their own design specifications for their parts. Not our engineers, the hourly employees. It's just amazing. Ten years ago, even though we had made a lot of improvements by then, we still had 2,000 defective parts per million, even though that was a lot better than 10,000 defective parts per million that we had at one time. We've since made remarkable improvements. You know what our defect rate is today? It's only **six** *parts per million. That's world class. When I first arrived there, there were around 10,000 people. Now, with only a couple of thousand people, we're one of the most productive plants in the U.S. We're one of the safest plants in America, too. It's a crackerjack organization.*

Trust Tips Dos and Don'ts

Do:

- Do identify your strengths and talents.
- Do build on your strengths and talents by serving your community.
- Do pick one person today whose expectations you can exceed—pick another person tomorrow.
- Do approach you career as a lifelong learning opportunity.

Don't:

- Don't avoid additional developmental opportunities outside your current areas of expertise.
- Don't forget that you can learn new skills.
- Don't brag about what you can do, demonstrate it concretely instead.

Next, we define the fourth piece of the ROCC of Trust – Compassion.

6

Compassion: The Fourth Piece of the ROCC of Trust

It is not the credential one has that matters...it is the concern one shows. - Seen on the office wall of Dr. Elizabeth Sherertz, MD, MBA

The final piece in the ROCC of Trust is Compassion. Compassion at a minimum is not taking advantage of another party. At higher levels it means demonstrating genuine interest in the needs of another; and at its highest level it includes altruism.   It also requires empathy, for it isn't passion about *something*, but for *someone's* needs and concerns. We leave Compassion for last because we really can't trust someone fully without knowing if they truly care for us. Even if they are reliable, open (and honest), and competent, we may not know if they have any concern for our well-being. For a trust-based relationship to last, it must also be based on mutual concern for one another's interests. This is the essence of compassion: does this person have our best interests at heart?

Compassion typically takes the longest amount of time to develop of the four pieces of the ROCC of Trust because not only do we have to discover what the needs of another person are, but we also have to find ways to meet those needs. Sometimes we even need to make sacrifices to fulfill those needs. Before even learning about others' needs, however, we need to first acknowledge our own biases, assumptions, and selfishness, and listen empathically as Steven Covey states in *The Seven Habits of Highly Effective People*. We will discuss at length empathic listening as a way to build trust later in the book.

Learning about a person's needs takes time because people do not freely discuss their needs unless they trust someone, so it is almost a Catch-22: I will not divulge my needs to you unless I trust you, but I cannot trust you unless I feel that you understand and are concerned about my needs. That is why openness typically develops before compassion—as a leader, we can be open about our own needs and concerns and lead the way for others to share theirs, as well. Once that they see that we feel comfortable enough to make ourselves vulnerable, they then are more willing to open up with us as well.

Bob Lintz and Removing the Ties that Bind

Bob Lintz once told Aneil's Executive MBA class, "Why are there unions in this country? Because people were abused." Bob himself was abused plenty by his superiors in his career. It helps to explain why we've never seen Bob wearing a suit, a blazer, or even a tie. It is clear that Bob wants to dissociate himself from the managers and rules that made life miserable for him and for those around him for much of his GM career. Ties are symbolic of the chokehold that GM management had over hourly and salaried employees for decades, which stifled the initiative and creativity of more than tens of thousands of people. From the very beginning of Bob's career, he was determined to remove that stranglehold.

The very day after he graduated from Michigan State University, he started working at GM. He received only a one-day orientation. Given that it was June, and many of the supervisors were on summer vacations, his first job was as a "vacation supervisor replacement." This is how

Bob relates his initiation into full-time corporate life at the largest manufacturer in the world. "I'm a supervisor of about 30 people. My knees were shaking. If you'd had had a pair of castanets attached to them, I would have sounded like a John Phillip Sousa band." His superiors used intimidation to get work accomplished, not only with the hourly employees, but also with the salaried supervisors, too:

I was sent home one time because I wore corduroys. I was sent home another time because I wore a blue shirt. You've got to wear a white shirt if you're in management. You've got to have a white shirt. That's the good guys – the white shirts. I was sent home once when my hair was too long, because I looked like a Beatle. Management couldn't drink coffee out in the plant. So what you'd do is go to a coffee machine and hide in some little obscure area and suck down your coffee and keep your fingers crossed you didn't get caught. You learn how to survive in this atmosphere even while being intimidated.

At the end of the first year, only four of the nine college graduates stayed, and I was one of the four. Quite honestly, there were an awful lot of days I'd go home to my wife who I'd just married right of college, and I'd say "I don't know if I can handle this." I eventually (decided) that I was going to stick this out and I'm going to make a change. The change that I visualized in those days was a better working relationship with my people.

Bob decided to use a different approach. He decided to trust the people that typically weren't viewed as trustworthy by his peers and those above him: union employees. As he moved up the managerial ranks, Bob developed a philosophy of collaboration with the hourly people and the UAW, which he called the TEAM concept.

Prior to Bob's becoming plant manager, the relationship between union members and management had been win/lose—if one side won on an issue, the other side took that as a loss. Parma's previous management team had refused to put doors on bathroom stalls! It also had required employees to use "hall passes" to get between different parts of the plant. In one of the worst examples we were told about during our interviews with the Parma employees, we heard about when hourly employees had regularly asked for water fountains in the plant, because the summer heat inside a stamping plant in the Midwest can be unbearable. After years of asking, the Human Resources Manager finally acquiesced and installed the water fountains. The big day came for the unveiling and when one of the employees went to turn on the first fountain, no water came out. The HR director was standing close by and was heard to say, "You requested a fountain, but you did not say that you wanted water!" No plumbing had been installed.

In the early 1980s, Bob faced a situation in which his $250 million Parma, Ohio stamping plant would be shut down in three years, and more than 6000 employees would lose their jobs. His plant was rated as one of the worst within GM in terms of quality, productivity, and costs. There was also significant overcapacity within GM, making it highly unlikely that corporate management would want to invest in the plant. In a facility represented by the UAW, Bob had no ability to alter wages or benefits, and could not make unilateral changes as to how work was done in the plant in any effort to improve productivity.

In the end, Bob's compassion for his plant and his people won over those who were cynical. As we will find out later in subsequent chapters, Bob's compassion, demonstrated though creating a revolutionary open door policy, empathic listening and humility, led his employees, both hourly and salaried to an impressive turnaround of the plant. One of our favorite stories about Bob and the Parma plant comes several years after the turnaround effort had begun to succeed. Bob was walking through the plant and happened upon an employee he didn't recognize.

We had a new line of robots going into the plant. I'm looking at it and here next to it is a guy in coveralls, who are usually our skilled tradespeople like electricians. I said to him, "Are you associated with this line?" "No, no." He said, "Say, aren't you Bob Lintz?" I said, "Yeah." He said, I just came here from Atlanta, Georgia." He keeps on getting closer and he's right in my face, right here. "This is the worse damn plant I've ever worked in." He went on about how hated the union and he hated General Motors. I've learned in my career never to stoop to that level, so I just sit and listen to this guy blow off. His face is beet red. He gets all done and I said to him, "Are you married, by chance?" He said, "Yeah, yeah." I said, "Do you have children?" He said, "Yeah." And, I said, "You know, your blood pressure must be about 1000 right now." I said, "If you've got this much hate and animosity about working for this company, I would expect you probably take this home to your family." "You must have a miserable existence." He replies, "Well, I hate this company." I said, "Well, you know what I do if I was you?" He says, "What?" I said, "I'd quit." I said, "'Cause you're going to kill yourself. You're going to die of high blood pressure or a heart attack." He said, "I've only got five or six more years. I'll put up with it," and walked off. I was pretty pleased the

*way I handled that, by not losing my temper with the
employee.*

Later that day, Bob happened to be walking through
the plant on the way to meeting. For the first time in
many years, the Parma plant was in the process of hiring
people from outside of General Motors to fill 100 new
jobs. To remove any politics as to whom might be hired,
each Parma employee was given one job application which
they could give to a relative or friend. The job
applications would be randomly selected, and then
applicants would be formally considered for one of the
new jobs.

*That particular day was the day when there were going
to be 1,000 applications handed out and if you wanted to
get in line to get an application for a friend, you could do it.
A lot of people were lined up in the Personnel Section to get
the form. As I'm walking by, here's this guy in line for a
job application, the guy who had just read me the riot act
about what a lousy organization we were and how much
he hates the place. I know he saw me, because when he
saw me, he kind of scooted into the wall a little bit. I just
keep on walking, so I'm not late to my meeting. I walked
down about another 100 yards and decide I've got to find
out why a guy who hates our company this badly would
want to get a job for anyone else. So, I turn around and*

walk back. He knew I was coming. He was trying to hide. He was wedged right into the wall with his head against the side of the wall. I said, "Say, you and I just had this discussion about what a lousy organization this was." He never turned around and looked at me. I said, "Who are you trying to get a job for?" I'm asking you a simple question." I heard him mumble, "my son." I said, "I couldn't hear that, could you tell me a little clearer who that was?" He said a bit louder, "my son." The moral of the story is that even though a lot of people like this guy had to behave in way that demonstrated their apparent dislike for the organization, deep down this guy knew that it was a helluva great place to work, and that he would be very fortunate to get his son into Parma.

Trust Tips Dos and Don'ts

Do:

- Do surprise someone by remembering their name or something special about them.
- Do spend 5 minutes listening to someone today, and see how it makes them *feel*.
- Do ask someone what you can do to help *them*.

Don't:

- Don't create artificial barriers based on your title or your position.
- Don't spend more time focusing on your own needs over those of others.
- Don't waste time focusing on how you've been wronged. Instead focus on how to make it right without hurting others.

II

Building the ROCC of Trust

7

Keep the Door Open

An open door invites callers. - Turkish proverb

Keeping an open door is an active extension of being open. It consists of a set of behaviors that invite others to share their opinions, concerns, and ideas with you. It is more than a suggestion box, and is not simply allowing people access to you. It conveys the idea that you are prepared to listen and that you will take action based on what you hear. Just because you open your door doesn't mean people will start coming in to see you. If other parties don't know you or have reason to distrust you, it may take a while before they come knocking. Nevertheless, keeping the door open by itself helps you to demonstrate Reliability and Compassion. Once they do start visiting you, how you listen and take action allows you to demonstrate Openness and Competence.

Bob's Open Door Policy

Bob Lintz decided that he had to demonstrate that he could be trusted, and that he had begun trusting the UAW leaders. Roger Montgomery, Shop Chairman for many of the years that Bob led the Parma plant, credits Bob's sincerity and openness with their ability to respect each other and work together for the good of the plant and its jobs. Roger felt that he had been able to put aside his past doubts of management's sincerity and work with Bob to create an environment based on teamwork and trust.

Bob decided that he had to overcome the distrust and misconceptions about what he and the management team wanted to achieve at Parma. He also felt that there was not enough dialogue across the hourly and salaried staff in his plant of 5,000 in Parma, Ohio. Because much of the distrust was between hourly employees and their supervisors, Bob felt that he had to take the lead in removing some of the barriers between management and the hourly employees. He eliminated the separate parking and dining facilities for hourly and salaried employees.

He also wanted his employees to feel comfortable talking to him and so he instituted an Open Door policy. This policy meant that whenever an employee—any employee—came to his office, he would stop whatever it was that he was doing and listen to that employee's concerns. He wanted his workforce to know that he was serious about open communication. Bob took his open door policy so seriously that when we were interviewing Bob for a case study we were writing about him and the Parma plant, he asked us to leave his office when a group of employees came to see him. We regularly witnessed his Open Door policy in action on this and many other occasions.

He extended his open door policy by getting out of his office as much as he could and spending time with the hourly employees where they worked. He walked around his plant, regularly stopping to shake hands with his employees who numbered several thousand, asking them how they and their families were doing, as well as what he could do to help them in their jobs. He also removed the status barrier between hourly and salaried employees, and set an example for the managers and supervisors that reported to him, by getting rid of his suits and ties, typically wearing a sweater or golf windbreaker and slacks instead. As a result of these and other efforts, the employees could see that Bob was really serious about open communication, and they in turn became serious about communicating back to him.

An ongoing challenge of this Open Door policy is that as Parma improved its operations, it began to receive employees who were being transferred from other GM facilities that were being shut down. Over 1700 employees were transferred to Parma from other GM plants over a ten-year period alone (1987-1996). According to Jay Dillon, the plant's HR Director during this time period, "the biggest challenge was taking these 1700 transplanted employees and integrating them into the Team Concept, and refreshing management people about the concept." The challenge was to sell this Open Door policy to GM employees who had never worked under such a policy and were deeply suspicious of management in general because they had been repeatedly transferred in order to keep their jobs somewhere within GM. Additionally, after a 20-year period during which it was previously not allowed, new people who had never worked for GM also began to be hired beginning in 1998. These new hires also had to be integrated into a system of open communication. In addition, Parma, along with the rest of General Motors, continued to downsize through attrition and early retirements and buyouts. Bob had to continue to work hard to sustain the trust with the remaining employees even as the plant faced relentless pressures to improve quality, cost and productivity.

Over the last decade of Bob's tenure as plant manager, machine efficiency improved 200%, and labor productivity in terms of volume produced per employee improved four-fold between 1990 and 1999, when Bob retired. Quality, cost and productivity have continued to improve under Bob's successors, and Parma has been rated the #1 stamping plant throughout GM worldwide since 2004 in terms of these three critical performance areas.

One unintended consequence of Bob's Open Door policy, however, was that the salaried supervisors and managers felt that their authority was undermined by allowing hourly employees to go over their heads directly to Bob. Moreover, these salaried employees didn't have the same job protection or benefits as the UAW-represented employees, and faced a greater threat of downsizing. Once he realized this, Bob began to focus his efforts on building trust with his management and supervisory employees as he had done with the hourly employees. Even though he couldn't promise them the same type of job security, he did initiate several significant training initiatives, including a Supervisors College, which enhanced their skills, made them feel part of the Parma team again, and removed barriers between hourly and salaried employees at levels below Bob.

As a result of Bob's efforts to build trust between management and the hourly employees and their union, the Parma plant not only received new products that kept it open, it has now grown into a billion dollar enterprise. Bob's passion for his work and his compassion for his people and his willingness to "open his door" resulted in one of the most dynamic organizations within GM, one that continues to thrive to this day.

Trust Tips Dos and Don'ts

Do:

- Do make it known that you have the time when people need it.
- Do set aside a specific amount of time each day and week to get out of your office area to "bump into others."
- Do document your conversations so that you can follow through on them.

Don't:

- Don't allow distractions to interfere when people come to talk to you (e.g., checking email).
- Don't forget to include employees at all levels in your open communication.
- Don't create artificial barriers that prevent others from working together (e.g., designated parking or eating areas).

Bob taught us how to open our doors to listen to others. The next step is to listen with your heart.

8

Listen Deeply

Empathy is probably the most potent factor in building rapport with people, in achieving an accurate understanding of their thoughts and feelings, and in eliciting their cooperation both as individuals and in groups. - Carl Rogers, *A Way of Being*

For us to build the ROCC of Trust, keeping the door open also requires another capability: listening empathically. Hearing with your heart involves more than listening—it requires that you put yourself in the other person's shoes and think from their perspective. It is easy to say we are "listening", but when we hear with our heart, we are demonstrating our compassion about the person and their thoughts and feelings. It can involve a significant sacrifice of time on your part, which is one way you can demonstrate your compassion for another person.

Careful Listening

The Rev. Jean R. Smith is a great example of an empathic listener. She just retired as Executive Director of the Seamen's Church Institute of New York and New Jersey (SCI.) Trained in Speech Pathology and ordained in the Episcopal Church in 1980, Jean has demonstrated a unique ability to listen to others' concerns with an open heart and an open mind. She has applied this ability, which she originally used as a priest, into successfully transforming and leading a major not-for-profit organization with a global reach.

One of her subordinates, the Rev. James Kollin, who serves as a chaplain for SCI, described her ability to listen deeply:

I worked as a social ministries coordinator and as a children's ministries coordinator for eight years in my home diocese in the Philippines. Somewhere along the line I asked my bishop for further studies and he gave me an application for an internship at SCI. I was accepted as an intern for a 9 month course in New Jersey. I was homesick and wanted to go home after the first 3 months. Jean said, "Do you have family in this country?" "Yes, I have two sisters, one brother. One in New Jersey, two in Philadelphia, one in California. She said 'Would you like to talk with them? She encouraged me to get in closer touch with them during my time in the states. She also challenged me to use my own homesickness to focus on the feelings of foreign seafarers who are away from family for as much as 12-14 months. That's how I managed my homesickness. I stayed and finished the internship. After my training I went back to the Philippines and after six months Jean e-mailed me asking me if I wanted to be an SCI chaplain. I thought about it and talked with my bishop and family and they said "go ahead." So, I came back to the States and we have been here now for six years.

To me, Jean is first and foremost a coach. She addresses problems immediately and provides and proposes solutions quickly. She inspires, she encourages. I've been with leaders many times before where it's hard when no one makes decisions and nothing happens for fear of making mistakes. Another one of Jean's staff members, Ann Mills, works from Paducah, Kentucky on a ministry project serving river mariners. She told us that Jean is a "colleague, not a boss," and described her leadership style as "beyond phenomenal." Ann said that "Jean believes in you until you give her reason not to."

Jean herself described her leadership style and approach to working with her subordinates in a very similar manner:

What I especially enjoy about this work is the necessity to make it new every day. That doesn't mean we have no policy, that we have no established programs, and that the strategic plan is out the window. It does mean that the way we implement the strategic plan may be different from the way we did it yesterday. Today's shipping is heavily regulated by security codes and plans which may and often do change overnight. Our chaplains must reach the mariner and respond to their needs. In this atmosphere it is essential that our chaplains are encouraged and empowered to be creative and focused on solutions.

Jean trains ministers to focus on listening to the needs of those mariners they serve:

How we understand their request for social services, legal assistance or spiritual support, and how we respond depends upon our careful listening, without pre-judging or making assumptions. The men and women we serve come from some 70 nations and represent many different cultures and religions. They are living on a ship and away from home for months at a time and may be easily exploited. They deserve our knowledge of the industry in which they work, our thanks for their labor, and our best listening skills. It is essential that chaplains listen to and act on what is being said, not what they may want to hear. When a mariner says, "I need your prayers" and the chaplain responds "Would you like to receive the sacrament?" the chaplain may be told "No, I gave that up long ago, but I do need help collecting overtime pay." If this is what we hear, we know what to do, how to help, and fully believe this, too, is ministry.

Building trust, then, can begin with listening deeply and hearing from the heart.

Trust Tips Dos and Don'ts

Do:

- Do look into the other person's eyes when they are speaking—give them your full attention.
- Do clarify their thoughts and feelings to make sure you understand them correctly.
- Do take the time so that you can fully understand other points of view.

Don't:

- Don't interrupt until they are finished speaking.
- Don't be impatient when others want to share their thoughts and feelings.
- Don't be defensive when others are sharing their feelings.

The next chapter outlines how these leaders not only know how to listen, but how they know how to put themselves in another's place to understand their perspective.

9

Put Yourself in Their Place

You never truly know someone until you've walked a mile in his shoes. - Anonymous

You may have an open dialogue with someone and discover that their opinions vary greatly from your own. In order to have truly open dialogue, you not only have to open your ears and your mind, you must also open your heart. In other words, you have to listen in a way which requires not only cognitive ability, but emotional capacity as well. Once again, this requires inner security on your part, because much of what you may hear may run counter to what you have heard before, or what you may think yourself is correct, and may require you to change your own behavior. As Covey writes in *The Seven Habits of Highly Effective People*, the paradox of trying to influence others through empathy is that you may yourself be influenced.

Create a Safe Place to Speak

Once you have opened the conversation with someone, you must provide a safe place for them to express views that are different from yours, where they know that they will not be criticized for them. Bob Lintz decided that the only way to get good decision making from his staff was to encourage this type of open dialogue at staff meetings and to encourage an exchange of opinions that were different from his. When his staff made decisions, they were not Bob's decisions, but the staff's decisions. That meant that when the group left the room, they were all in agreement about the direction the team was to take. That also meant that the discussion leading up to that agreement might not be so agreeable. Bob was willing to admit that he did not know all of the answers which is why he preferred to gain consensus with his top management team. He recalled that there were times he left a management meeting batting 0/7 in agenda items, despite walking into those meetings thinking that he knew the answers to every issue. He said it was very humbling to him, but that he knew it was the right way to lead his team.

Listen at Lunchtime

Bob also provided a safe place for the local UAW representatives and hourly employees to speak their minds. On example of this was when a General Motors executive vice president was scheduled to visit the plant to hear a presentation by a joint union/management team that Bob had put together.

By this time, we had gotten the UAW really on board. We had told them everything about cost. We told them how much it cost for steel, how much the labor costs were. They knew everything we knew. We had an executive vice president coming from General Motors who we had to sell on our turnaround plan. Our hourly and salaried people would be presenting it to him. It was going to knock his socks off.

Well, the day before he was to arrive – he was supposed to be there at 9:00 in the morning – his secretary called me and said that he's got a schedule conflict. Would it be ok if we rescheduled him to 10:30 in the morning rather than 9:00? I'm thinking, oh, boy, that's lunchtime but what the heck. I want the guy here. Well, with the limited time that he would have, by the time we gave him the presentation and got him out on the floor, these people would be at lunch, so he really wouldn't get to see the spirit of the hourly organization. I decided to move up everybody's lunch an hour early, so that when the executive vice president came here, we'd still have an opportunity to get him out on the floor. Pretty good decision, right?

I think at that time we had 5,000 people. All they've got to do is move their lunch hour up an hour so that the EVP can come out on the floor and see the plant humming and everybody making good parts. That's all – a brilliant decision on my part, right? It didn't take me long to come up with that great idea (Bob indicates how long by placing his first two fingers on his right had about a centimeter apart). I ask my secretary, Mary, to type up the announcement, and she printed up tons of copies to be distributed throughout the plant. The plant's about three million square feet in area, so back then it took a while to get the message out to everyone.

About a half hour later, a union leader comes in to me. 'Bob,' he said, 'you don't mean this, do you?' I said, 'yes, John, there's been a change of schedule. Everyone will have to move their lunch up a little bit, so the EVP will still get out there and see all of them at their jobs rather than just eating lunch.' 'Bob, Bob, Bob," he says, 'You will never convince 5,000 people that they have to adjust their regular daily routine for one man.' I said, 'John, come on. You're kidding me.' I said, 'We've come a long way.' He says, 'We have come a long way, Bob, but we haven't come that far. Trust me. They will be really mad at you for doing something like that.' I said, 'But, John, this is for all the jelly beans. You know, we've got a half a billion-dollar project here we're trying to sell to General Motors.' He said, 'Bob, it won't work.'

I'm not a union guy. I didn't grow up in a union family. There are lots of times I can't understand the way they've developed their attitudes and value systems. But at this stage of our relationship, I'd learned that I had to listen to these guys. So, I told John that I'd get a new bulletin out and we'd change it back to the regular schedule, but I also told him that it was a shame that we couldn't show off the plant while it was in full operation. He said, 'Bob, this is the only way you can do it. We'll have to take our chances.' So, I told Mary to issue a new announcement that we would be having our usual lunch time.

I then called the EVP'S secretary and told her that while the rest of his visit would be as outlined, he wouldn't be able to see all the people at work because of their lunch schedules. She said that that would be a shame, and I agreed. She then said, 'Well, I'll tell you what, I'll move his schedule around so that he comes to Parma at 9:00 a.m.'

So, he did end up being able to see our people working after all, and as a result, we sold the project! The story very quickly got around the plant, too, that I had gone out and fought for the people.

There certainly was a real learning curve to my ability to listen to others. I'm pretty proud of the fact that I listened to the UAW. I could have been the good corporate soldier, and fallen in line with whatever the EVP could do or couldn't do. Instead, by I was able to show that we managers and the UAW were really listening to one another.

Trust Tips Dos and Don'ts

Do:

- Do be prepared to change direction based on what you hear.
- Do let others lead you when they see the big picture.
- Do get out of the way once you've empowered others.

Don't:

- Don't let the hierarchy get in the way.
- Don't forget that you're just one person even if you are the leader.
- Don't fail to communicate the changes to everyone involved.

The next chapter explains how to go where you're needed, even if it means leaving the comfort of your own office.

10

Go Where You're Needed

Develop a genuine interest in and concern for other people. - Zig Ziglar, 1991.

Leaders demonstrate compassion in another way by going to meet with their followers and colleagues on their own turf. It shows courage by getting out of your own comfort zone and protected territory. It demonstrates humility because the act of visiting someone else shows respect for what they have achieved and what they can teach us. We have already discussed how Bob Lintz did this with the UAW, when he was the first plant manager to visit the Local UAW headquarters.

Get out of your comfort zone

The four leaders of Two Men and a Truck, International routinely do this as well in their regular visits with their franchisees. It started informally under the founder Mary Ellen, as many of the franchisees were her friends. She would report on her visits with these franchisees in the monthly company newsletter, always ending the report with a bad joke that she had picked up on the road. It became more formalized when all three of her children started working for Mary Ellen at the Home Office, freeing up time for Mary Ellen to make these visits. As Mary Ellen delegated more leadership responsibilities to Melanie and the Two Men, Brig and Jon, and as the number of franchisees grew, these three began doing more of the visits.

Those early visits under Mary Ellen provided the opportunity to demonstrate compassion and openness with her franchisees. She would find out where the franchisees needed assistance in their operations, especially in the area of training. Over time, with visits by her children, the visits became more structured and focused on implementing best practices, holding franchisees accountable to the franchise contract, as well as providing technical assistance in business management. These efforts emphasized the need for greater reliability and competence, and helped the franchisees to build these pieces of the ROCC of Trust. These visits also allowed the three siblings to build relationships with the franchisees as had Mary Ellen, but with their own authentic styles.

These visitations were a key part of the strategy to professionalize the franchisees who often had little in the way of formal business backgrounds. These visitations not only built relationships with new franchisees, but also brought a human face to Melanie's efforts to rigorously enforce the franchise contract that several franchisees had stopped adhering to. Two Men and a Truck, International also created the position of field consultant who was responsible for visiting each franchise twice a year as well as providing on-call assistance. This position was especially important whenever a new franchise was launched. As one field consultant told us, "I would say there is a high level of trust out there in general between Home Office and the franchisees, otherwise, I think the field consultants would be on the road a lot more to really follow up on issues." These efforts have created double-digit growth for the franchise system for more than two decades, where the average revenue per franchisee has grown more than 40% over the past six years, and now exceeds $1.3 million/franchisee.

Trust Tips Dos and Don't

Do:

- Do set appointments and follow-through.
- Do identify who are the important people you need to visit.
- Do bring the attitude that you want to learn from others.

Don't:

- Don't create status barriers between you and the other party.
- Don't forget to share what you learn from your visits with others.
- Don't forget to thank the other party for sharing their time with you.

The next chapter describes the importance of learning to ask for help as a way to build trust.

11

Humbly Ask for Help

I really don't know a great deal about what I'm supposed to do, and I'm going to have to rely on you folks to help me. - Bob Lintz as a new supervisor

Asking for help is an important way to build trust, but it requires humility because you need to acknowledge that you don't have all the answers. Because of this, it also means being willing to be vulnerable, because others may interpret a request for help as a sign of weakness. The paradox then is that in order to build trust with others, you must often be willing to trust them first. To reinforce people's behaviors, you also need to develop a "grow the pie" culture in which others believe that they will succeed with you, not despite you.

A wonderful way for leaders to demonstrate both courage and humility in order to build trust is by **asking for help.** At the beginning of his GM career and throughout it, Bob regularly asked those around him for help in ways that built trust in him and provided the foundation for building trust in one another. One of the reasons that Bob found it so easy to ask for help from his subordinates is because he himself would have benefited from help of his peers and bosses when he started out at GM, but he didn't receive it.

In the 1960s GM was just starting to integrate college graduates as manufacturing supervisors. The day after I graduated from college, I began working at GM to replace other supervisors who were taking their summer vacations. I had 30 people working for me from day one.

Management assumed that I knew everything because I was a college graduate, but I really had no idea what I was supposed to do because I'd only received a four-hour training program. I would try to talk to my fellow supervisors, but because I was a college graduate, and they weren't, they wouldn't talk to me. Instead of having college degrees, those supervisors got their jobs because they were the best at telling people what to do by cussing at them.

On the other hand, the hourly UAW people, the ones who worked for me, went out of their way to help me. It didn't take long before I realized that the good guys were the hourly employees. As their new supervisor, I had told them that "I'm going to have to rely on you folks to help me." My hourly employees really liked being asked for help. At the time, I was too naïve to understand how different I was from the traditional guy who came up through the ranks, and later I realized how critical it was to influence others in the organization by simply asking for help.

When asked recently what some of the turning points were in transforming the Parma plant into a team-based culture, Bob mentioned this example:

The regional head of the UAW had the wisdom to ask me to address all of the hourly people in a union meeting, even though that had never been done at General Motors. Management people were simply not allowed at union meetings. We couldn't have a union meeting in the union hall, however, because it wouldn't hold all of our thousands of hourly employees. So we did it at our plant, basically shutting it down and setting up big speakers. The regional UAW guy introduced me as having an important message, the reality of our business. I start to give my presentation and start hearing all these catcalls from throughout the plant, 'Get him out of here. Get him out of here. No management people in a union meeting.' It got to a point where I couldn't even speak any longer. So, the regional guy gets up and he says, 'give the man an opportunity, he's trying to help you.' For a union leader to talk about a management guy as really sincere and trying to help was unheard of.

Bob's act of going to the Union Hall was also an act of vulnerability because while he was the boss in the plant, the UAW membership had ridiculed him many times on his own turf, so it was very likely that when Bob went to their meeting, they would be emboldened to act even more negatively. His willingness to expose himself in this manner led the way toward his building a more trusting relationship with the Union at the Parma plant.

In this and other ways, the local and regional UAW leadership gave Bob an opportunity. Bob also gave them the same opportunity to articulate reasons why the plant needed to change the way it operated. The local UAW, with support from their UAW bosses, provided him with a trusted platform, the union hall meeting, to talk about the state of the business, and to articulate how everyone would have to work together if Parma was to win new business and avoid certain closure.

Trust Tips Dos and Don't

Do:

- Do be willing to admit you don't know everything.
- Do be willing to trust others first.
- Do encourage everyone to find common ground.

Don't:

- Don't be afraid to ask for help.
- Don't forget to include everyone's point of view.
- Don't be afraid to tell the truth in order for people to really understand the state of your business.

12

Set High Expectations

It's human nature to defer the most challenging changes. Leaders often emphasize the tactical rather than the strategic. This delay distracts the organization from the urgent need for change. These same leaders will eventually be discussing 'the need to start soon--as long as everyone is ready' from their rocking chairs at the retirement home. - Dave Schecklman, Oshkosh Truck Corporation

Having had the courage and humility to empower others by asking for help, it is important that the leader set high expectations, which also demonstrates courage. When a leader sets high expectations, he or she is depending on others to have the capabilities to achieve the goals that have been set. That is courageous because of course it is always possible that people won't rise to the occasion, won't have the proper background, or won't be quick enough even if they do have what it takes.

In asking for help from his hourly employees, Bob Lintz not only communicated a set of high performance expectations, but also the process that would generate the results. This process was to be a partnership between unionized hourly employees and non-unionized salaried managers and staff. Setting such high expectations, however, would not have worked if the ROCC of Trust had not been first established by Bob with the local UAW leadership, and through them the hourly employees, and ultimately the entire Parma organization.

As part of his collaborative approach, and even though he knew it would be more time-consuming, Bob decided to form a joint union/management team to develop new business in hopes of keeping the plant open. Most GM plant managers at the time would not have delegated such an important task, instead keeping it within their management teams. Bob knew, however, that if this plant had any hope of surviving for the long term, the entire plant membership had to take ownership to ensure its survival. Before it could even come up with ideas to save the plant, this joint team first had to develop a set of rules and guidelines so that they could work together productively, which they had never done before. Bob also ensured that they would receive the necessary training and support as they learned how to analyze data, make presentations to outsiders, and accept criticism when their work wasn't good enough.

Once this team had developed a joint operating philosophy, they began working together to identify areas in the plant where they could take on new business. The Parma plant was an internal supplier plant to other General Motor's plants, so hourly and salaried employees went out together on the road, making joint presentations about their capabilities to other GM plants which were their customers, and to GM's top brass. They quickly found out they weren't even competitive with other GM stamping plants, much less the Japanese. As Bob told us:

This place was a disaster. From the start, having the union leadership accept what the real world looked like was essential. We invited some of the union leaders to sit in with our engineering team, and they would help perform the studies on new product opportunities. They would go through all the numbers, the generation of cost of material, the cost of labor, overhead costs and all the things associated with developing a product. Even after all of this joint work, which they were proud of, they found out that they didn't get the bid for new business, because the numbers weren't good enough. So they got a real dose of reality. Through continual efforts to redo their business processes and redesign the way in which the union and management worked together, the joint union/management team at Parma eventually began to submit proposals that were competitive, and thus began to win the new projects that rescued the Plant from closure.

Get Others to See the Big Picture

As the plant began to win new business and improve its productivity and cost competitiveness through its collaborative approach, Bob then found himself faced with a situation that threatened to undo all the success that Parma had achieved. When a new local UAW shop chairman, the head of the union bargaining group for Parma, was elected to replace the retiring Roger Montgomery, he brought with him a list of over 650 demands. In contrast, Roger Montgomery had worked with Bob, the local UAW and the Parma's management team to reduce the number of demands to an average of 100 annually over the previous several years. As Bob told us, and as we know from our own experience, however, one of the ways in which local UAW leaders get elected is by identifying needs and wants among the workforce and by promising to fulfill them.

Before we had this new guy with his 650 demands, the local negotiations with the UAW had become almost kind of predetermined. We knew together where the organization needed to be and what things we needed to do. Roger had had to demonstrate his leadership as a union leader by coming up with demands, but they were good demands. They were things that if I were the union leader I'd be doing the same thing. Well, all of a sudden, I've got 650 new demands, including a swimming pool and a baseball diamond. Parma's scrambling to stay alive and we've got to deal with this. I get about halfway down the first page of demands, and I'm just sick because I know that Roger's successor didn't come up with all those ideas. He just went out and asked everyone to give him their wish lists.

Why did Roger's successor act the way he did? He was politicking. He happens to be an extremely bright, gifted guy, but he thought it would be good for his image to give into anything that the hourly employees demanded. Roger would have refused, but his replacement, who was new to his leadership position, couldn't say no to anybody. He thought he was doing the right thing, but didn't see the downside when management refuses to agree to demands that are quite unreasonable and that wouldn't be consistent with our transforming Parma into an effective operation. The local UAW leadership was going to have to explain to their membership why they didn't get everything they'd been promised.

We could have embarrassed Roger's successor and just trashed the demands really quickly. The other approach was to sit down and organize all of the demands in a way that we could have a win for everybody, jointly identifying what the most important demands were. I think the key is that I actually went to him and I told him that. I said, 'we're going to sort through these things and make you look as good as we possibly can, knowing that we aren't going to agree to most of these demands.' He agreed, and we were able to negotiate in such a way as to allow the union to do its job and still help the plant continue to improve. They didn't get a swimming pool, but they got what was necessary for both sides.

When Roger's successor actually moved on to the International UAW, he never forgot Bob's willingness to not embarrass him by refusing all the demands outright. From then on, anytime that there was an opportunity for this union leader to do or say something to either the UAW leadership or top GM management that was good for the Parma organization, he did so. He turned out to be a great ally of the Parma plant.

Trust Tips Dos and Don'ts

Do:

- Do be willing to set the bar high.
- Do encourage the talents of others, especially those that complement your own.

Don't:

- Don't overreact when someone throws you a curveball.
- Don't embarrass others even as you demand what's necessary from them.

The next chapter explains how we can create trust by making work a game in which everyone can participate.

13

Make it a Game: Ted Castle and Rhino Foods

It is an equal failing to trust everybody, and to trust nobody. - English Proverb

Coach Instead of Control

Ted Castle, President of Rhino Foods, is someone who refuses to constantly look over the shoulders of his employees. His background partly explains his leadership philosophy. He earned a degree in environmental sciences from the University of Vermont. He played hockey while in college, then coached hockey and played it professionally in Sweden and Italy, and he was also Assistant Hockey Coach at the University of Vermont and University of Maine.

"Going to school in the '70s, everyone in college was against business, and making money was a bad thing. So when I left coaching to go into business, I decided I was going to make it a worthwhile endeavor where we could make a lot of positive change. That's what turned me on, and still does.

In 1981, he and his wife Anne had concocted an innovative dessert, two chocolate chip cookies sandwiching vanilla ice cream custard, known as Chessters, which was an immediate hit at the ice cream and deli store they had opened in Northern Vermont. Despite this initial hit, and later broader business success, his humility still is evident when he describes how he came to build a multi-million dollar food business. *"I ended up in business because I didn't get the head coaching job at the University of Vermont (UVM). My wife and I had already started a tiny ice cream store, and at least I could go work for my wife when I didn't get the UVM coaching job."*

Going to work for the store wasn't a lot of fun initially. *"I would be selling ice cream cones at the counter to people who would be regularly asking me, 'Aren't you supposed to be the hockey coach at U-Vermont?'"* Luckily, we started *doing a wholesale business so I could focus on making cookie dough for my wholesale customers and not have to keep hearing that question all the time."*

While the business was growing but still small, Ted had to make use of equipment owned by his friends. *"I would take my cart with all my cookie dough ingredients, eggs, flour and sugar, up the elevator to use a mixer in a restaurant owned by my friend. After that, I would then take the cookie dough mix across the street to a grocery store to use its ovens to make my cookies. Then I'd come back and make my little ice cream cookie sandwiches, wrap them up and put them in my car and drive across town and put them into customers' freezers. That was the business plan to overcome my embarrassment that I didn't get the top coaching job!"*

On one of these days when he was transporting his cookie dough ingredients to mix them, the elevator door opens, and as he pushes the cart out, his tray of 30 eggs falls out of the cart and breaks. The eggs start to ooze toward the crack between the elevator and the floor. Three ladies are at the elevator door, waiting to get on, and they give a questioning look at Ted, as if to say, do you know what you're doing? In recalling this incident, Ted said *"I think things happen in your life for a reason. That's when I decided I had to grow my wholesale business so that I could afford my own equipment and wouldn't have to keep spilling eggs everywhere in front of people"*

Even as Rhino Foods continued to grow, Ted realized, and others noticed, that his heart wasn't really into it the way he had demonstrated in his coaching career.

Someone he had begun working with in the business said to him, "Business is going all right, but you don't really have a passion for it; you're still embarrassed that you're not the head hockey coach. You better figure out how to do this like you do most things, which is to go after them pretty hard, or you should just get out of it." He and this colleague determined that there really wasn't much connection between his former coaching work and his current business practices. Ted's experience playing and coaching hockey provided the inspiration for how to grow the business in a way that would be more motivating to himself and to his employees, and that we would argue is based on the ROCC of Trust.

Make Work a Game That All the Players Can Win

Ted developed a management philosophy based on his hockey experiences in which he had learned that coaching was a better approach to managing his people than monitoring or controlling them. He decided to motivate his employees by having them set high standards for themselves and their work and holding themselves accountable to those standards.

While coaching and playing hockey he had learned that playing a game, and winning, was a highly motivating way to achieve. He then adopted a team-based, game-oriented approach to running Rhino Foods. *"I have a fundamental belief that most people like games, and they don't have to be football players or hockey players to enjoy games. People can like bridge, or checkers, or Risk, or Monopoly."* He developed a list of things that people like about games:

You know your opponent, you know the beginning and the end, there's usually a time-frame, and you know the score. If you win, you usually celebrate. If you lose, you usually feel bad and try to figure out what to do next time. You meet and you prepare. What was there about Rhino Foods like that at the time – nothing! Then I thought, wouldn't it be interesting to try to bring the elements of a game into our business? The score is making money. It initially sounded scary to share profit information with our people. But my colleague said, how would feel if you played a game for three hours with scorekeepers and at the end of the game they blew the whistle, closed the scorekeeper book, and didn't share the score with you? That's when I decided to take a chance and open up our books to the 20-25 people we had back then. That's the how The Game really started.

In several ways, the management philosophy and approach that Ted developed not only demonstrated his trustworthiness in terms of the ROCC of Trust, but also demonstrated his trust in his employees. Rather than acting like a hall monitor, regularly checking on his employees to see if they were playing by the rules, working hard, and performing, he established instead an organizational structure, reward system, and culture that demonstrated the ROCC of Trust to his employees. In the process, these organizational characteristics served to enhance his employees' trustworthiness, which made it easier for Ted to make himself more vulnerable to them, i.e., place greater trust in them.

He first demonstrated Openness by allowing every employee access to the operating performance (e.g., expenses) of the company, and he demonstrated Reliability by posting this information at Rhino Foods each day. *"The reason we did it daily is that we think that the most current, the most specific information is the best for people."*[2] This information sharing also required some courage on his part. *My biggest fear was that people were*

---

[2] Ted Castle's visit to Aneil's MBA class, October 29, 2002.

going to think I'm making myself rich. But, I knew I wasn't getting rich. We were making money, but at times I thought I could be making more money mowing lawns again. So I said this issue should be easy. It comes down to whether you're willing to be open.

For example, before Ted's open-book management approach, employees thought that if they made four batches of fudge batter brownies, the company would be able to sell it for about $7,600, and that most of that selling price must be profit. By opening the books, however, he was able to show that half of this amount had to go to pay for the ingredients alone. He itemized all the costs for his employees, and then showed them that the company also had to pay 40% in taxes on the amount that remained after all the costs had been paid for. He showed them that the company would only be profitable if they had done all their work correctly. *"I would remind them that 'last week we did it wrong and we had to throw it all away'. I would then ask them what might have gone wrong with that job. So we just started sharing information, and once you do this, you build confidence. It's contagious. If you want people to act like owners in your business, you just tell them what you know."*

Talk Like Ted

Ted Castle of Rhino Foods emphasizes how communicating creates fun, and through this fun, building the ROCC of Trust by demonstrating his humility, his courage, and his authenticity. As he told us, *it's our purpose and principles that we believe in that are important. We're trying to help people listen and respect each other, while engaging them by making it interesting. To a group of 130 people who just got off a seven-hour shift at 6:00 in the morning, I'm not going to show 20 PowerPoint slides.*

Interestingly, creating fun-filled communication is a serious business according to Ted:

We believe it's everybody's job to figure out how to engage people, so we look at it as a teacher does. There are good teachers and there are bad teachers, and the ones that usually are considered better engage their students. We take really seriously that we need to be able to communicate in a way that grabs people's attention, having some fun along the way usually grabs people's attention. Sometimes, when we want to celebrate something, or when we report the first-time quality, the performance schedule, or our safety record, we have more fun by showing a picture of me with my Rhino hat on and my thumb up or thumb down. The people that have to do the reports thought that it would be really funny. So they flip the picture up and I'm either wearing a frown on my face with my thumb down or I'm with a happy face. It's not really about me; instead it's about how our employees have chosen a way to engage with me and with one another in a way that they can laugh about.

This approach to communication, coupled with substantial job training and business education, enhances his employees' own Reliability and Competence, by making it easier for Ted to delegate more decisions to his employees. *"Personal responsibility is something we spend a fair amount of time talking about and figuring out how to make that happen."*[3] By creating a reward system in which employees participate in a profit-sharing arrangement in Rhino Foods

---

[3] Ted Castle's visit to Aneil's MBA class, October 29, 2002.

once the company's capital investment requirements have been reached, Ted not only demonstrates Compassion, but he also increases his employees' trustworthiness by aligning their interests with those of the firm.

Another way in which Ted Castle demonstrated his trust in his employees and his Compassion for them was by loaning out his employees to other local firms needing seasonal help when Rhino Foods went through a downturn. The idea to allow employees to work at other firms in fact came from the employees themselves, when over half the employees brainstormed over a period of three weeks on ways to avoid layoffs at Rhino. Ted asked his best employees to volunteer for the Employee Exchange Program to ensure its success, and Ben and Jerry's was one of the firms to sign on to the program.[4] In exchange, he would guarantee them their jobs once the market picked up. This innovative approach to downsizing and seasonal demand fluctuations could only work if Ted had 1) built a trusting relationship with his employees and 2) Rhino Foods had credibility in the community.

As the business has grown, so has the need to change how Rhino Foods shares information with employees. "The Game" is now played differently. As Ted Castle recently told us, *"we've continued to work hard at sharing information,*

---

[4] *Managing with Lou Dobbs*, CNN, March 18, 1995.

helping people know what's critically important for our business." An annual planning process is now in place, with annual bonuses provided for achieving goals. With three shifts running, the company now has three sets of company meetings on the same day each month so that everybody can come. Annual goals are reviewed, as well as any financial information that employees want to talk about. For 2007, four performance items "critical to the business" were tracked: performance to schedule, first time quality, safety, and customer service levels. As Ted put it, *"the concept of looking at the business, seeing what's important, sharing the information, tracking daily results, getting people motivated to improve on those numbers has continued."* The Game evolves from year to year, based on a number of factors, with Ted recognizing the tradeoffs between familiarity with and complacency about performance indicators, and between flexibility and efficiency:

How we do it each year is based on what's important, and how savvy our workforce is. We tend to do introduce new metrics carefully, because we find that when we bring out a new metric it takes awhile to gain some traction. So to be constantly changing things every year doesn't make sense. We've measured performance to schedule, first time quality, and now we're measuring safety differently. We keep some of the old measures and then move some of the new in as we try to focus on different things. The reason for why we play The Game, however, has not changed. We still believe it's important to have a daily focus on activities. In some part of the organization we're actually shortening the feedback time period. The production floor has an hourly performance worksheet. The three different lines they're running know what they're supposed to make every hour now and they're measuring whether they did so, and if not, how we can fix it right away?

In further refining his approach to sharing information, Ted recognizes the critical importance of providing feedback based on the nature of the task, and not using a "one size fits all" approach:

The concept is to be identifying the most important things to the business, but also what is the right amount of time to be tracking it, how can we be adjusting it? We've really gotten into this idea from Toyota: "plan and do, check, act." It's a continuous improvement methodology; we need to be picking the right plans to be tracking, how we go about checking on them and how do we go about adjusting them. If we make the problem so big that we never get to do it then we're never going to get anywhere, so the concept is we're trying to keep getting better at little chunks.

As Ted Castle has increased the level of trust throughout the organization, he has fostered the flexibility, creativity, and even patience that is so essential to any organization. At Rhino Foods, there no longer is a need to reward people every week based on their performance, and Ted can even wait to *share* some of the performance information with his employees, and wait to reward them for their performance, even as such information still gets *measured* daily:

We've combined our monthly bonuses into a six-month bonus, but we're still measuring our goals daily. We're still reporting progress on our goals at each monthly company meeting, but then rewarding our employees based on achieving these goals every six months. We continue to mature, grow, and figure out what works best for us, but the concept of sharing information, trying to get people to understand that they have a way to impact those results is what is really important.

Rhino Foods' performance has vindicated Ted Castle's coaching philosophy. Rapid growth began in the 1990s based on selling inclusions, e.g., brownies and cookie dough to major ice cream manufacturers like Haagen Dazs and Ben and Jerry's. In addition to making and selling the Chessters ice cream cookie sandwich, they also make ice cream novelties and desserts for some of the largest food companies in the U.S. They have more than tripled their employment since the early 1990s, growing from 40 employees to 140 by 2007, and revenues have grown even faster, reaching a peak of $30 million in sales in 2005, and remaining roughly at that level through 2007. This is a significant achievement, especially as Rhino Foods co-packs for very large national companies, and the firm operates a highly competitive segment of the food industry where not all new ice cream products have long product life cycles, and not just because they melt!

Ted and Anne still own 100% of the business, but they are *"not running the business to go public or to sell it. Instead we are doing it because we still enjoy it, and because we're trying to create a really interesting work environment where people enjoy coming to work, where people are challenged, and we are following our Purpose, Principles and Vision, doing good things.* [5]

---

[5] Ted Castle's visit to Aneil's MBA class, October 29, 2002.

Trust Tips Dos and Don'ts

Do:

- Do give yourself a new title: Coach.
- Do find ways to share more information with your employees.
- Do create a reward system which encourages everyone to win as a team.

Don't:

- Don't be a hall monitor.
- Don't create incentives for people to work at cross purposes.
- Don't be stingy in sharing the fruits of your success.

The next chapter explains how trust is built slowly over time by being clear and consistent in all of your communications.

14

Be Clear and Consistent

I think that we as leaders have an obligation to be clear and consistent. We need to tell people what we're telling them, review it again with them, and then review it with them one more time. Then, we need to do this all over again the next day. - Dennis Quaintance

Dennis Quaintance, Partner and Co-Head of Quaintance-Weaver Enterprises, a hotel and restaurant firm, puts the leader square and center in communicating and building Reliability within an organization. It means connecting rhetoric to behavior, values to actions, and purpose to priorities, and repeating it in a way that is neither boring nor insincere.

If you wander around in any of our businesses, we not only have our mission statement up on the wall, but also the concrete actions that connect it. Here's ours:

To provide the highest quality food and drink at a good value, provide prompt, friendly, attentive service by a well-trained staff in a clean, comfortable environment, provide an outstanding menu plus an impressive selection of specials. To provide employment that is rewarding, and offers education and opportunity. To generate profits that justify the investment, allow the organization to grow and to allow compensation to those who contribute.

Even though ours is pretty simple, it still is pretty general. So, right next to that is, "Wash your hands often." Because one of the problems with most mission statements is they're ridiculous. How can we provide the highest quality food and drink if after eating in our restaurants you go home and puke your guts out because someone didn't wash their hands?

Dennis has found a way to build the ROCC of Trust by simplifying the goals of his firm and the expectations for his employees and by sharing information openly and consistently about whether those goals and expectations are being met.

Trust Tips Dos and Don'ts

Do:

- Do communicate your goals and purpose to your employees and your customers.
- Do make sure your behavior is consistent with your rhetoric.

Don't:

- Don't forget the details that support your goals and mission.
- Don't forget to make your expectations concrete.

The next chapter encourages leaders to create a lasting organization by not worrying about the future, but instead putting one foot in front of another.

15

Put One Foot In Front of Another

She won't leave. They never do! - Mary Ellen Sheet's former boss at the State of Michigan

After working for the State of Michigan for twenty years, Mary Ellen realized that if she wanted to break through the glass ceiling, she would have to create her own building. During the time she worked as a systems analyst for Michigan's Department of Social Services, four different men she worked with were promoted to supervisory positions. Meanwhile, management ignored her successful work on harder projects than those performed by the guys they had chosen to promote instead of her. Managers expected that she would never leave her job. Such an attitude "made it very easy for me to quit and run my little five-truck moving company."

Mary Ellen Sheet's company, Two Men and a Truck, which operated those five moving trucks in 1988 had actually begun several years earlier. Her two sons, Jon and Brig, had begun moving furniture in the early 1980s as a way to make money during high school using an old green pickup truck the family had purchased from Michigan State University's Grounds Department. They placed an ad in the local Okemos paper, *The Towne Courier*, with copy written by their mother which simply said "Two Men and a Truck". She also drew a simple logo for the business — a stick figure of two happy men driving a truck.

Years later, she remarked that her two boys, Jon and Brig, *"weren't really men, and the truck was 'borderline.'"* The stick men logo she had hand-drawn for the business, was on the moving sheet used for each move. They only made one copy of the sheet for each move because "they never wanted to leave a copy with the customers. In case they broke something, they didn't want the customers to know who they were!" Jon and Brig charged $25 an hour. They each kept $10, and five dollars was put in an orange dish for advertising and gas expenses. As Mary Ellen told us, if Jon and Brig had saved up enough for their needs, or their friends were throwing a party, but the boys had promised to do a move, "they would call up the people and say their truck had been stolen! They were teenagers, after all."

Despite the less than customer-friendly tactics, the business did well and when Brig and John returned to Northern Michigan University in the fall, people kept calling to have their moves done. Mary Ellen decided to keep operating the business by hiring two men to help her with the moving. By May of 1985, she bought a used truck that cost her $350. After work each day as a systems analyst for the State of Michigan, she would return home, listen to her answering machine and schedule moves for Joe and Elmer, her two movers. She would charge the customer $25 an hour, pay each man $10 an hour and use the rest for gas money and placing classified ads. At the end of her first full year in business, she had made a $1000 profit. Not wanting to have to figure out how to pay taxes on the income, she simply gave the money away, writing ten $100 checks to charitable organizations.

She started franchising TMT after attending a MSU conference on entrepreneurship in 1988 at which a lady who owned a pet care business and had franchised it told her to do the same. "That same month, I met with Ray Damas, and he said he would help me franchise the company. She quit her State of Michigan job as a computer programmer and systems analyst, and in 1989 she awarded her first franchise outside the state of Michigan to her daughter Melanie Bergeron, who was a pharmaceutical sales rep in Atlanta. Her son Jon also became a franchisee, in partnership with his mom initially, and friends of hers also became early franchisees. In 1994, she asked her daughter Melanie to help run the franchising headquarters operations, known as "Home Office," when she was asked to run for a state-wide office by the Michigan Republican Party. Melanie became president. Her brother Brig sold his franchise in the fall of 1996 and moved back to become vice president. Jon served on the board along with his mom and siblings.

As the enterprise grew, led by the four family members, it developed a number of practices, governing mechanisms, and reward systems that helped to create a solid ROCC of Trust. Unlike many entrepreneurial firms that grow into large companies, TMT, International has managed to avoid the rigid bureaucracy that often accompanies growth. Indeed, TMT International has found a way to retain its entrepreneurial roots and vigor while systematically building the organizational structure and formalizing the culture in ways that enhanced the ROCC of Trust.

TMT International builds Reliability throughout its franchise system in several ways. First, it has instituted standardized moving practices and processes in an industry that is known for poor reliability (e.g., never exactly knowing how much you'll end up paying for a move, or when the movers will show up). Home Office insists that franchisees pay their royalties each month on time. Trucks must all be white with the black logo, no exceptions, and movers must dress neatly. Customer feedback is collected by Home Office from each move and fed back to the franchisees in order to maintain consistency and dependability across all franchises.

Home Office develops Openness by publishing a monthly newsletter for all franchisees and conducts an Annual Meeting for all franchisees. The company also has created an on-line information system in which any franchisee can obtain operating performance data about any other franchisee. These communication outlets enable franchisees to learn about success stories and suggestions for improvement from one another.

Through its hiring and performance evaluation practices at Home Office, Competence is demanded and rewarded. All new employees must go through an initial 90-day probationary period of employment, and performance-based pay is part of employees' compensation. If franchisee employees earn perfect scores on customer feedback forms, they receive a cash bonus, and cruises are awarded to top-performing franchisees each year.

TMT International has built Compassion through its annual meetings in which franchisee successes are celebrated and company values are shared through stories and examples from the four family members and all the franchisees. Home Office employees are compensated at above-market rates, to not only attract and retain the best employees, but also to demonstrate that it is not only the four family members who benefit from the success of the franchise system. Indeed, Melanie made it a point to let employees know that the Jaguar she drove to work was paid for by the profits from her own franchise, and not from her salary as President of the company. TMT International's Stick Men University demonstrates Compassion in three ways, by enhancing the capabilities of franchisee employees, by showing in a visible manner how some of the franchisee royalties are being spent by Home Office, and by helping to ensure that customers' goods are moved safely and without damages. Home Office sells all of its Pro Shop merchandise to franchisees at cost so that they are encouraged to have all their employees wear clothing with the TMT logo.

By placing her trust in her three children, as well as in her employees, in twenty years, Mary Ellen has created an enterprise with annual revenues that in 2007 exceeded $200 million. Mary Ellen has earned the trust and admiration of her employees and her industry, as evidenced by being awarded the 2004 Entrepreneur of the Year by the International Franchise Association for her vision and savvy. She was the first woman to earn this award in its 40-year history. She achieved this success by putting one foot in front of the other.

Trust Tips Dos and Don'ts

Do:

- Do surround yourself with people you can trust.
- Do find sources of stamina to draw upon when faced with difficulties.
- Do find ways to continually improve your products or services.

Don't:

- Don't be fearful of trying something new.
- Don't forget to invest in your employees so that they can help you grow.
- Don't neglect to put the right team in place that can journey along with you.

Next, we profile leaders who excel at giving others hope for the future, which is critical in any journey we undertake to build the ROCC of Trust.

16

Help People Hope

It's my job to be your optimist. - Brent Senior, M.D.

The common theme across the following four physicians is that through their outstanding Competence in their chosen specialties and their abundant Compassion for their patients, they are able to provide optimism to their patients and are willing to partner with them to develop innovative treatments and procedures. They are all excellent listeners. Their empathic listening enables them to know the whole person, not just the body part they are treating. As a result, they are trusted by their patients and their colleagues.

The Optimistic Otolaryngologist

Dr. Brent Senior is an Associate Professor and Division Chief for Division of Rhinology, Allergy, and Sinus Surgery in the Department of Otolaryngology Head and Neck Surgery (ENT) at the University of North Carolina at Chapel Hill. Ms. Barbara Esterly is a Registered Nurse who works for Dr. Senior in the Department.

One of the most important gifts a leaders can give their followers, and a physicians their patients, is hope. Dr. Senior and his partner, Nurse Esterly have helped to give me and my family hope many times, and often when we most needed it. I first came to Dr. Senior in 2002. This was three years after I'd had a sinus surgery performed by another otolaryngologist, a surgery that had left me far worse off than before. That surgery had resulted in several symptoms which I'd never had before, including a severely dried-out nose, constant sinus pressure, and over time, chronic daily headache.

Before seeing Dr. Senior, I had seen several different ENTs, and had even traveled to the Mayo Clinic, but no one was able to help me get better. Finally, an ENT who had tried his best but was stumped recommended that I travel to Chapel Hill see Dr. Senior, who he thought very highly of. In desperation, I made an appointment with him and sent him my detailed history that I had written.

I teach my MBA students that effective leaders have to be courageous, humble, and authentic. These three characteristics in turn allow leaders to develop the trust with others that is essential to creating lasting change. I have found this to be true with physicians as well, and Dr. Senior is one those physicians who has helped to teach us this. It takes courage as a physician to assume responsibility for treating patients who have failed to improve under the care of other healers. It also takes a great deal of humility on his part as well, for he has had to try a great deal of ideas out over the years as we work to repair my damaged nasal passages, and when some of these ideas don't achieve our desired outcomes, new ones have to be developed. Finally, his authenticity is apparent as he acknowledges his own disappointment when my progress is not what we'd like, he reaffirms his determination to keep working with me, and when he demonstrates his good humor, not only when I when I complain about my nose, but also when our beloved Michigan Wolverine football team disappoints us the previous Saturday afternoon.

Dr. Senior and Nurse Esterly both exemplify the ROCC of Trust. They are nothing if not reliable. In the countless appointments I have had with them over the past six years, they can both be depended upon to be efficient, thorough, and respectful, and to be available for follow-up questions if need be. While doing everything he possibly can on my behalf, Dr. Senior has also been open and honest about the challenges of dealing with what is basically unknown territory for both of us. I have benefitted many times from his surgical skill and diagnostic expertise, but as I prevail upon him to help me alleviate my condition, Dr. Senior has reminded me more than once that he will first do no harm. Nurse Esterly's quiet professionalism is actually quite amazing. I have rarely seen someone work so hard, so humbly, and so generously. She actually blushes when I thank her. Finally, both Dr. Senior and Nurse Esterly have demonstrated compassion that I have typically only seen with loved ones. During one of my lowest moments, Dr. Senior said to me that "it is his job to be my optimist." Nurse Esterly has also always been there for me as well, returning my phone calls promptly and reassuring me when she senses that I am anxious. I am truly blessed to have these healers in my midst.

The Holistic Healer

Dr. Alan Finkel is Professor in Neurology at the University of North Carolina at Chapel Hill, specializing in headaches and pain management. Karen Fisher is his nurse, and the one who takes all the initial patient measurements such as blood pressure and pain self-assessment. Dr. Finkel's hallmark is thoroughness, as he spends as much as 2 ½ hours with new patients during their initial appointments. Subsequent appointments may last anywhere from 15 minutes to 90 minutes, depending on their symptoms and progress. He simply takes as much time as necessary for each appointment. Some of the words that patients use to describe him are: intense, intellectual, caring, funny, sardonic, curious, sympathetic, and highly intelligent.

Dr. Finkel enjoys taking the time to educate his patients on the many issues, study results, and ambiguities that surround the field of headache and pain management. In teaching his patients, he maintains a direct but engaging style. He is highly collaborative with his patients in his efforts to understand and treat their often quite complex medical problems. He constantly seeks input and opinions from his patients, asking them to reflect back on and even question the views he expresses. He can be quite humorous without ever disdaining or discarding his patients' concerns. Patients note that it is not just his expertise and rigor that brings them back, but his effective listening and caring manner. Dr. Finkel looks at the whole person when diagnosing headaches, looking back at their life experiences and how those might have shaped their headaches. He is also a highly positive person, regularly providing encouragement to patients when they are feeling discouraged about their headaches or other symptoms. He works with them until the proper dose and type of both preventive and pain medications are prescribed.

The major downside of his attentive approach is waiting time. It is not unusual to wait an hour or more past appointment time to see him, as he often goes over the allotted time for each patient that he sees. In addition, the waiting time to get a follow-up appointment with Dr. Finkel can sometimes take several months, reflecting the strong demand for his expertise. His nurse, Karen, however, is adept at fitting in patients who have immediate needs to see Dr. Finkel. A vital partner in the care of Dr. Finkel's patients, Karen is also an empathic healer, and can be counted on to discuss whatever their patients like to before they see Dr. Finkel, or simply to be a great listener to people who need to be reassured and encouraged. Her empathy for patients who are suffering and her enthusiasm for healing others coupled with Dr. Finkel's own competent and compassion manner make for a powerful combination for healing others.

The Adult Pediatrician

Dr. Bruce Rubin is Professor and Vice Chair of Pediatrics at Wake Forest University Baptist Medical Center (WFUBMC), specializing in pediatric pulmonology and mucociliary clearance. Bruce is an excellent listener, and a fair magician to boot, both of which come in handy when he works with his young patients. His nurse, Kay Ashburn, is an important part of his care team, responding to patients' inquiries, scheduling tests, facilitating examinations, and occasionally handing out chocolate to well-behaved patients. Kay's energy and optimism are, dare we say, "infectious," and help to make all of the patients who see Dr. Rubin, especially those who are have chronic diseases such as cystic fibrosis, feel more hopeful.

Aneil found Dr. Rubin because our kids at the time went to the same school, and Karen remembered Dr. Rubin's license plate—MUCUS. Aneil had significant and worsening problems clearing mucus following sinus surgery and was desperate for any insights into his conditions. Dr. Rubin and Aneil chatted amiably at a school open house, and after hearing about his difficulties, he encouraged Aneil to come see him for a formal evaluation. Even though Dr. Rubin conducted research relevant to Aneil's problems, he went above and beyond his duty because his clinical responsibilities at WFUBMC were pediatric and not adult. He would be adding to his workload without any additional resources or recognition from his bosses. In essence, he would simply be taking time out of his very limited personal time to help Aneil.

Over the course of the past nine years, Aneil, Dr. Rubin, and Nurse Kay have forged a collaborative professional relationship and have become good friends. Initially, Dr. Rubin and Aneil got to know each other better through their clinical interactions, then socially. Through these interactions, Dr. Rubin came to appreciate more and more fully that Aneil needed his research insights, his clinical expertise, and his friendship. Dr. Rubin has investigated new drugs, novel procedures and solicited clinical trials participation on behalf of this patient in an effort to alleviate his chronic condition and ultimately heal him. Nurse Kay has partnered with Dr. Rubin in suggesting one particular procedure to Dr. Rubin for Aneil's condition. Dr. Rubin then forwarded on this possibility to Aneil's ENT who decided it was an excellent idea.

Aneil for his part, has tried to reciprocate the attention and concern that Dr. Rubin and Nurse Kay have shown to him. As a business school professor, Aneil encouraged

Dr. Rubin as he sought to pursue an MBA to complement his medical education and training. Dr. Rubin thought that earning an MBA would help in his leadership and management roles that come with being an administrator as well as a physician, and Aneil agreed. Dr. Rubin completed his MBA at Wake Forest University, and has put it to good use in his career. During each of his visits, Aneil also takes the time to discuss with Nurse Kay the challenges of taking care of so many very ill patients with chronically poor resources including insufficient staffing.

Whenever there is a new receptionist on the 7th floor Pediatric Admissions desk, the person always does a double take when I say, "yes, the appointment is for myself." Aneil is proud and grateful to tell the staff at WFUBMC that he is Dr. Rubin's oldest "pediatric" patient.

The Cardiovascular Change Agent

Kevin Lobdell, M.D. is Director of the Adult and Pediatric CV Critical Care, and is Associate Director of the Cardiothoracic Residency Program at Carolinas Heart and Vascular Institute in Charlotte, North Carolina. Trained as a cardiovascular surgeon, Dr. Lobdell had to redirect his career path when an accident prevented him from continuing to perform surgery. He found his niche in streamlining surgical care and has optimized a process for improving the time cardiac surgical patients are extubated after surgery by over 100%, and now as many as 80% of patients are extubated within 6 hours. He has achieved these life-saving outcomes and operational efficiency after realizing that his employees could be focused on a specific goal through his sharing as much data as possible with them. In addition to sharing data widely with fellow physicians, nurses, respiratory therapists and other staff members, he focused his energies on building these individuals into a cohesive team with a common goal. This effort was not only time-consuming, but took considerable energy for this self-described introvert. Dr. Lobdell drew upon multiple talents in order to create a sustainable organizational change effort. He has distinct talent in relentlessly finding out about and using information regarding treatment modalities, organizational processes, and clinical research to improve patient outcomes and well-being. He also has a strong talent in seeing interdependencies among health care personnel, patients, and technology. He is also impatient and intolerant of excuses when it comes to helping patients who would otherwise have to wait for resources and personnel to become mobilized for their welfare and even survival. When he combines these talents with his experience and skills as a cardiovascular surgeon, he brings a unique leadership strength that is critical in the fast-paced, high-stakes health care setting in which he works. His ability to lead teams and communicate quickly and concisely has led to this improved extubation rate and overall quality improvement, resulting in reducing mortality by nearly 50%, sepsis by 50%, and acute renal failure by 37.5%. It is noteworthy that these results also correlated with improved operational efficiency by reducing ICU and hospital length of stays.

Dr. Lobdell acknowledges that conflicts will arise in this journey toward patient improvement, but that as long as he and his team are all in agreement about the outcomes, the conflict will be worthwhile in developing trust and commitment to the common goal. Communicating honestly, direct, and humbly has been important to address this conflict directly. Humility comes naturally when improving outcomes for his very sick patients often comes slowly and only after months of hard work. He works hard to break down barriers between his M.D. degree and those who are not physicians, or even barriers between himself and other physicians who have been trained and rewarded over the years to focus their energies on their own agendas. One way in which he does this, and one which we resonate with, is through informal communication, and in particular discussing his colleagues' children. This reinforces his authenticity, as he is indeed responsible for a number of very sick child patients in his unit. Dr. Lobdell has found this to be an important way for him to demonstrate his compassion for his team and for them to find a common ground with each other. This common ground has enabled them to trust each other more, and take that trust into making their patients better much more quickly.

These physicians are trusted leaders due to their willingness to listen, to apply their expertise in the face of long odds and without expecting any reward, and their great compassion.

Trust Tips Do's and Don'ts

Do:

- Do learn how to be a good listener.
- Do spread optimism in discouraging situations.
- Do be an advocate for those who are most vulnerable.

Don't:

- Don't forget to take the time get know the whole person.
- Don't forget that your employees and colleagues are people as well as professionals.
- Don't neglect to address group conflict and its sources.

The next chapter illustrates the power of outrageous courage in building trust with others.

17

Be Outrageous and Courageous

All the world's a stage,
And all the men and women merely players:
They have their exits and their entrances;
And one man in his time plays many parts,

As You Like It, Act II, Scene VII
William Shakespeare

When communicating to others to build the ROCC of Trust, preparation is critical, and covering the "five w's" is essential. To demonstrate Compassion, it is essential to know *who* your audience is, especially their needs and values. Comprehending *what* to say *when* builds Competence, by emphasizing the most essential points succinctly so as to not waste people's time. Understanding *where* to deliver your message increases Reliability, so that your followers know how they interact with one another to deliver consistency and predictability. Perhaps most important, stating *why* you're taking others' time to deliver your message builds all aspects of the ROCC of Trust.

Dance Like Dennis

Dennis Quaintance likens effective communication to a play, with its actors, props, fanfare, and most important, rehearsals. As he readied his latest project, Proximity, which is the highest-rated Platinum LEED-certified hotel in the United States, this is how he described it in an extemporaneous speech to our MBA students when they visited the hotel only a few days before the hotel's grand opening:

We're actors who are both serious and silly. Our role is to cause delight in a sincere way and to take really good care of our guests. We do this paradoxically: we're serious about causing delight, but we're also light hearted in how we go about it. Our guests expect us to be competent and friendly. We achieve this by hiring authentically friendly people, who will be friendly no matter what sort of situation they're in. We expect our staff to treat the guests the way they themselves like to be treated. We find out quickly that the sadomasochists don't stay long because their guests don't like them!

For several days prior to our official opening, my wife and I and some friends stayed here to conduct dress rehearsals until we were comfortable that it was ready for guests, like a preview of a play. We then had a fun kick-off meeting with 130 or so staff. We knew that we needed to do something different to get their attention. I've always believed that to get people's attention, you need to change their expectation of what a meeting is. We'd never do a meeting where I'd ask them to sit down, and then tell them how great this company is, because then they'd throw up because it's just so predictable. So for our kick-off meeting, I stood on that cantilevered registration desk that you saw when you came in.

Then we did a snake dance on the land that we own across the street in front of the pond. Then we had a rain dance.

Only after all of these activities did I actually talk about our culture. In this organization we really are in service not to other human beings, but to our intentions, our purposes and our values. In terms of priorities, we first serve our guests, then we serve our staff; and third we serve our shareholders. Fourth, we serve our communities by valuing diversity, and fifth we serve our communities through sustainable practices.

We're sincere about providing employment that is rewarding in terms of both education and opportunity. We're very sincere about making a profit. We're sincere about our commitments to our greater communities. We tell our employees to care about what they're doing, and have the courage to employ their enthusiasm. We say to them that if they can't courageously employ their enthusiasm, then they should go find something they do care about and go do that. We believe we can really make a difference through our sincerity.

Trustworthy leaders courageously act outrageously, but in an authentic way that encourages their followers to discover what can be done differently and better, in an ongoing collective effort to remake their organizations.

142

Trust Tips Do's and Don'ts:

Do:

- Do be courageous while being "outrageous."
- Do share your stories about your values and beliefs.
- Do encourage employees to share their stories.

Don't:

- Don't forget so share your passion about what's important.
- Don't assume everyone knows your expectations or goals.
- Don't forget to have fun while earnestly leading others to meet your organization's goals.

The next chapter is inspired by a lunch we had with Dennis Quaintance. After leaving a large tip, we asked him to explain why, because while the service had been good, it didn't seem to justify such a large tip. His explanation enlarged our way of thinking "thank-you."

18

Think "Thank-You"

*I would maintain that **thanks** are the highest form of thought, and that gratitude is happiness doubled by wonder.* - G.K. Chesterton, 1874-1936

Think and then say "thank you." This sends a message to others that they are important, that what they did was important, and that you appreciate it. We cannot say thank you enough to the people in our life. Never take anyone for granted.

Thinking thank you requires a sense of humility, in this case the idea that whatever successes you've had to date, you haven't achieved them on your own. Even before those successes have been achieved, it is

145

worthwhile to thank people who are contributing to the potential success of any project, customer relationship, or goal. Often the people that help you have thankless jobs or tasks which are nevertheless critical. It's not the big people that you need to remember to thank as they'll probably remind you themselves! It's your peers and subordinates, who rarely get the recognition or appreciation they deserve for contributing to a team effort.

When Aneil first started working at General Motors full time after college, he quickly learned to appreciate the clerical staff who worked with him in the Salaried Personnel Department. As a newcomer, Aneil had a hundred questions about what to do, where to go, and who to ask, and these clerical employees were invaluable in the information and assistance they provided. Having been a clerical worker himself during one of his two summers working for the State of Michigan's Department of Licensing and Regulation, Aneil knew how tedious but important such work was. He remembered to thank each of the GM clerical employees whenever they completed a word-processing assignment for him, or answered one of his questions. Unfortunately, one of his new colleagues did not. One day, Aneil witnessed what can happen when someone forgets to think (and act) thank-you. All word processing assignments were placed in an inbox, and work was drawn from the bottom of the inbox. When Aneil's colleague, "Steve," had a word processing project, Aneil saw the clerical supervisor take it from the bottom of the inbox, and move it right back to the top, which resulted in the work being done much later! People who may have little formal power or authority can nevertheless have a significant impact on your job performance, even when you don't know it.

Karen once started a personal thank-you campaign at work. She did not have direct authority over many co-workers but required their cooperation in making their customers happy. Whenever someone attended a meeting, devised a solution to a problem, or went out of their way to get an answer for her or their customer, she wrote them a quick "thank you" note. Even though she was the relatively new person at the company, Karen was amazed at how many people said thank you back. They had never been thanked before, and that small act that took a minute to say or write was a valuable gift.

More recently, Aneil needed to see Dr. Bruce Rubin for an appointment, but couldn't wait the several weeks it normally would take to see him for a "well appointment." He emailed Dr. Rubin's nurse, Kay, to see if he could be seen sooner, describing his symptoms. Kay called him within a few minutes, and managed to work him within the week. When Aneil got there, it seemed about as busy as usual in the main waiting room, but when he finally was brought into the inner waiting room, Bruce's other nurse, Barbara, let Aneil know that it was one of the busiest days they had had recently, with Bruce splitting his time between seriously sick in-patients who had been admitted to the hospital, as well as regular sick patients like Aneil who were in the out-patient clinic. Since it was around lunch time, Aneil asked if she had gotten the chance to eat lunch yet, and Barbara remarked "no," and also stated that on busy days like this, sometimes they didn't get to eat lunch at all. She also stated that once Bruce had worked from 4:00 a.m. until 4:30 p.m. without ever eating anything.

It was at this point that Aneil decided he should do something to thank these great people for always being there for him, and thank them in a way that might make their busy day a bit easier. He called up one of his favorite lunch spots in Winton-Salem, The Golden Apple, and ordered a lunch tray that would be enough to feed not only Bruce, Kay, and Barbara, but a few other staff people as well. It was around the restaurant's busy lunch time, and so he was told it would take a couple of hours to have the lunch delivered, but Aneil knew it would still go to good use when it did arrive. As he drove home after his appointment, Kay called him to tell him that the lunch had arrived, and that several people had been able to get something to eat as a result. Here is what Bruce emailed to him later in the day.

Hi Aneil

I have to write and tell you what a lifesaver that lunch platter turned out to be - both for body and spirit. We had some really sick kids in today both in hospital and in clinic. By 3 PM none of us had eaten and we were running nearly 2 hours behind. The sandwiches, fruit, and cookies were fantastic and plentiful. In fact, plentiful was salvation.

I hate it when I show up on time for an appointment and then have to wait forever to be called on. Most of the time we get our scheduling just right but on days like today when stuff happens, everything gets out of whack and we are all stressed. By 3 PM some folks had checked into my clinic 2 or 3 hours earlier and were going crazy waiting in tiny exam rooms with busy kids. I went into each room and said "I know that you have been waiting for a long time and I am deeply sorry. We have had some emergencies with sick children this morning and never caught up so I am hours behind schedule and I feel terrible about it. I will see everyone and take whatever time it needs to help you but please be patient just a while longer. If it would help you and you are hungry after all this waiting, one of our patients saw how busy we were today and knew that we would not be stopping for lunch today so he surprised us by ordering delicious sandwiches, fruit, and cookies for our clinic staff. We have grabbed our lunch on the run but we have a lot of great sandwiches and cookies left over and we would be very happy to share some of this with you while you wait."

Some patients and families were really hungry and took up the offer. They were really grateful. Others weren't hungry but after hearing this story, they all smiled. Despite having a bunch of patients wait hours to be seen, we did not have a single complaint and everyone was polite and thankful.

Aneil - you saved us again!

Bruce

Trust Tips Dos and Don'ts:

Do:

- Do be generous in thanking others for their help.
- Do find useful ways that go beyond the ordinary to thank others.
- Do recognize that everyone has an important part to play and appreciates being remembered.

Don't:

- Don't forget how easy it is to put a smile on someone's face.
- Don't fail to thank people regularly.
- Don't forget that others have hard days, too.

The next chapter reminds us that it is important to build trust by building partnerships with others.

19

Partners in Trust

Take very good care of my business and I'll take care of you when you're ready to move on. – Brig Sorber, President, TWO MEN AND A TRUCK, INTERNATIONAL

Unless a relationship is a two-way street, a head-on collision is inevitable. One of the organizations we've studied has been adept at avoiding such collisions, literally and figuratively. Since its founding, Two Men and a Truck has developed into one of the most open and honest organizations we've had the opportunity to work with, not only as researchers and consultants, but also as customers. Unlike many firms in the moving business, TMT has a very simple and transparent way of communicating with its customers, from the very moment someone contacts them to inquire about their moving services to when the move is completed. The price customers pay for their move is typically no more than 10% higher than the initial estimate, and, based on our own experience, can be lower than the initial quote.

A key to her openness is that Mary Ellen is one of the most humble and self-deprecating people we've ever met. This is despite her significant success in the business world, having turned that $350 investment into a $200 million company, and in an industry dominated by men. One way that she displays her humility is through her sense of humor about herself. When she spoke on the campus of Wake Forest University about how she interacts with her employees, one student asked her what it is like working with her family and whether or not they call her Mom or Mary Ellen. She replied that at work they call her Mary Ellen, which is what everyone throughout TMT calls her. Such humility is truly real, and translates into organizational practices both in the Home Office and among its franchises. Mary Ellen has an informal policy where employees feel free to talk with her about whatever is on their mind. Her column in the monthly newsletter to franchises usually talks about her travels around the country meeting with franchisees and interesting people, but it also typically concludes with a bad joke or "shaggy dog" story that leaves the reader groaning and laughing at the same time.

Such humility has been imprinted into TMT's DNA, as TMT insists that serving the customer be the focus, rather than Home Office or even fellow franchises. As part of this emphasis, TMT works hard to partner with each of its franchisees, instead of simply treating them as sources of revenue. TMT communicates exhaustively with each of its franchises through an extensive company intranet that encourages franchisees to communicate with Home Office and each other about their operating results, requests for assistance and advice, and offers to help one another. As part of this system, TMT utilizes its proprietary "Movers Who Care" software program, which integrates employee record-keeping, payroll, move scheduling, customer database, invoicing and correspondence. It was adopted by all franchisees back in 2001, having been developed several years earlier. Home Office also uses monthly newsletters whose content has grown in variety and depth each year.

The Competence piece of the ROCC, is continually improved upon through TMT's employees who are Franchise Business Consultants, charged with helping each franchise improve their operations. Franchise

Business Consultants are assigned 20-25 franchisees that they are responsible for visiting two times each year, as well as maintaining regular communication and providing advice as needed. Their role is to help each franchise get launched successfully, and then partner with them to help grow its business along the way. If they find an idea that works in one franchise, they share that information with other franchisees. One Consultant noticed that a particular franchisee used shrink-wrap to keep a couch in place while it is being moved. Word spread, and now each franchise shrink-wraps customers' furniture—without any extra charge. TMT's desire to please the customer and continually improve performance across its franchisees is so strong, that it has had to close two franchises because their customers were not being served at the level TMT expects. As Brig Sorber, President of TMT and Mary Ellen's son, told us, "if something good happens out there, all the franchisees gain, but if something bad happens out there, they all get hurt."

Another means by which TMT works to enhance performance is by partnering with top-performing franchisees through a council called the TEAM. As representatives of the best franchisees they are involved in efforts to help the entire system grow and then act as liaisons back to their fellow franchisees. Members of the

TEAM must have one year of experience with TMT and can serve no more than two consecutive two-year terms. The TEAM's mission is "to promote a unified partnership by communicating the vision and ideas of our brand and operating system in developing customer-driven solutions for increased market share." One of the TEAM's ongoing goals is to regularly monitor the effectiveness of communications with regions, same market area sales, customer satisfaction scores, mystery shopper scores, system-wide employee retention, and system-wide training participation.

TMT also seeks to enhance Competence by helping its franchisees to retain their most talented and productive employees as they grow their businesses. One way in which TMT helps franchisees do this is by tracking customer feedback about each move and sending this information back to each franchise so that the best movers and customer service reps can be recognized for outstanding effort. Another effort is through its *Stick Man University*, which Home Office established in 1989 to provide free on-going training for franchise employees. An extensive number of courses are offered, both for new and experienced franchise employees. Franchisees can also take advantage of Home Office's resource library of training videos, management best-sellers, and other educational materials at any time.

Franchisees themselves instill Competence by providing their own employees with many ways in which to develop their talents and contribute. Jon Sorber, Mary Ellen's other son, Executive Vice President of TMT and owner of three franchises himself, related how he created a new position for the manager of his Lansing operations, Rob Felcher, to reward him for his outstanding performance. He knew that this man was ready for additional responsibility, yet Rob as a newlywed was not anxious to travel as a field consultant, so Jon created a general manager position for him to watch over his two franchises in Grand Rapids and Lansing. A total of 33 franchisees got their start either working as an employee either in a local franchise or for Home Office. Twenty-six came up through the local franchises, three came from Home Office, and four others had experience in both places.

One common challenge facing franchisees is the need to provide growth opportunities to employees who want to go beyond the initial job of mover while at the same time retaining enough movers to facilitate the franchise's rapid business growth. Helping employees identify their goals and aligning them with the success of the franchise is critical. As Brig Sorber told us about when he owned his own franchise, before moving to Home Office full-time:

When I would hire movers, and they would come in for their interview, I would say, "I know your goal in life was not to be a mover. When you were playing cops and robbers when you were a kid, you didn't go, 'Ooh, can I be the mover?' So I would ask them, "What is your goal in life? Where are you? What do you want to do?" A lot of their goals are things that we can help them achieve. So what we tell them is, 'Listen, I know you don't want to be a mover forever. These are the different things that you're going to do in this job that are going to help you reach your goal, help you be better at what you really want to do: 1)deal with money, 2) deal with machinery, 3) deal with people, 4) deal with time A lot of different management things. Let's work on those. Take very good care of my business, and I will take very good care of you when you're ready to move on.' When they look at the job as a stepping stone as opposed to an end-all, it's totally huge. It's a mindset. Then, if you see a person that's a dead-end person, you don't want to hire those people. You can't change those people, and they can run like a cancer through your team. So it's really how you set the expectation during even the interview, and it's the same thing when you bring on a new franchisee. It's the same thing.

Trust Tips Dos and Don'ts:

Do:

- Do partner with your employees to help them achieve their goals.
- Do encourage employees to communicate with you.
- Do encourage employees to talk with each other to solve problems.

Don't:

- Don't forget that the customer's priorities should be your own.
- Don't neglect to share ideas that can help others in your organization.
- Don't think zero-sum; instead find ways for you and your organization to both win.

The next chapter shows us how to apologize appropriately when we inevitably make mistakes or hurt someone else.

III

Rebuilding the ROCC of Trust

20

Apologize Appropriately

Show me a man who cannot bother to do little things and I'll show you a man who cannot be trusted to do big things. Lawrence D. Bell (www.pprsites.tripod.com)

Restoring the ROCC of Trust *Does* Mean Having to Say you're Sorry.

Most of us find it difficult to apologize, mostly due to our own shame. But, if you discover that you truly are at fault, a well-spoken apology can do wonders for repairing and rebuilding trust in a relationship. Early in her career after earning her MBA from the University of Michigan, Karen found her policy of always being honest strongly tested. She was in a pre-negotiation meeting with Pepsi for several million dollars' worth of new business. This meeting was Karen's opportunity to build a partnership with Pepsi that would differentiate her company from its competitors, and an opportunity to increase its share of Pepsi's business from the 30% it held at that time. At this meeting, the customers provided a test of Karen and her firm's willingness to be honest by posing two very simple questions to Karen and her bosses: *'What is the new building we see down the road from our plant? Are you putting in a new production facility?'*

It was inevitable that Karen's plant personnel would eventually talk to the Pepsi plant personnel about the new facility, which was indeed being built close to Pepsi's plant in order to serve them better. After all, the plastic bottle business consisted of tight networks in which suppliers and their customer's bottling plants all knew each other well. What the Pepsi executives at this meeting did not understand was why they had to learn about this new facility from their own employees rather than from Karen's firm directly.

Even though Karen's largest and most important customer had not been properly informed by her firm about the facility, here was an opportunity to make it right, to proudly describe this new state-of-the-art facility and how it would help Pepsi. Karen was the least senior employee from her firm at the meeting, so she waited for her boss, the Director of Marketing, to answer the question. But Karen's boss chose not to do so, and instead actually *denied* that a new facility was being built, and then she moved onto other business.

Karen sat there dumbfounded. Karen knew that her boss had lied to other people before, but never in such a bold and blatant fashion, and she had not seen her lie to Pepsi before. In addition, her boss already had a reputation as a controlling and dishonest person, so this incident would only further strain the relationship with Pepsi. Karen could only assume that her boss didn't Pepsi the truth because she had wanted to surprise them with the news of a plastic bottle production facility to supply Pepsi's bottling plant. Karen, then, was put in an awkward dilemma—she could tell the truth, undermining her boss and probably losing her job as a result, or keep her mouth shut and lose the trust and loyalty she had worked hard to build with her customer.

During a break in the negotiations, Karen's boss left the room before Karen did. One of the Pepsi representatives looked at Karen and said, "Do you expect us to believe that you're not building a plant?" She realized then that she would probably lose her job, but because her customer's trust was very important to her,

Karen looked at them and simply said, "I'm sorry. I don't understand why she is behaving the way she is. We are actually building a plant to better serve your needs. I always want to be honest with you and I want you to be able to trust me in our dealings together." When the negotiations resumed with Karen's boss back in the room, the Pepsi representatives never said anything, but they never trusted Karen's boss from that day onward.

Not surprisingly, Karen and her boss never got along well but Karen was able to move on and work for someone else within the year. The best redemption for Karen was when Pepsi went to the General Manager of her Division and asked that she be their National Account Representative. Karen was the first female and the youngest person ever to be responsible for that $75 million account, which at that time represented half of the revenue for Karen's division. The General Manager of Karen's company told Karen that she was not his first choice, but that she was Pepsi's first choice. Karen's apology, coupled with her openness and honesty with Pepsi on a somewhat small matter resulted in Pepsi choosing to trust her on a far larger scale.

Being open and honest includes **apologizing** when you are wrong. We have found that some people find this difficult to understand. It may be because apologizing is often seen as a sign of weakness and so we are not encouraged in the business world to apologize. We nevertheless have found that apologizing is often a necessary and even first step in fostering open and honest communication when trust has been broken. Such communication is essential if trust can be restored. While the focus of our book is on how to build trust, the reality is that while trust can be robust, it quickly becomes fragile when mistakes or wrongdoing occurs without ready acknowledgment and making amends.

When apologizing, it is important to speak directly to the person with whom you have a problem. It is easier to talk about that person behind their back, but not only is that unproductive, it typically escalates the conflict and lessens the likelihood that we will restore the lost trust. Indeed, telling others about our conflict rather than the person directly involved is the opposite of openness and honesty. It demonstrates that we are interested in having others feel sorry for us or getting angry at the person who may have wronged us than in resolving the dispute. It is sometimes true that it is difficult to confront certain people we have problems with because of their unwillingness to listen or their basic lack of empathy. In these instances, which we believe are rarer than we might wish to think, we need to have the courage to still apologize and then move on, realizing that we'll never be able to fully understand one another. Still, we will have least apologized for how we may have wronged them.

Why is it so difficult for us to confront people when we have differences of opinion? One reason is that it is easy to assume that the differences are based on fundamentally different interests, when they may simply be due to much more superficially differing positions. We mistake a position for an interest. It is possible that we might just have compatible goals in mind, but have different approaches to getting there. We become so fixated with how we get there, that we forget to focus on the end, not the means to the end.

Trust Tips Dos and Don'ts:

Do:

- Do identify those who you have hurt, and try to assess what you could have done differently.
- Do be brave enough to admit when you are wrong.
- Do seek out people whose relationships with you need to be repaired.

Don't:

- Don't be afraid to apologize when you're wrong.
- Don't think that it is ever too late to apologize.
- Don't forget that trust is especially fragile when others are feeling hurt.

The next chapter reminds us to communicate more during a crisis, to keep the lines of communication open, and to demonstrate our compassion.

21

Communicate Clearly During Crisis

Nothing travels faster than the speed of light with the possible exception of bad news, which obeys its own special laws. - Douglas Adams, *Mostly Harmless*

An organizational crisis is any major threat to an organization's survival when there is little time to respond, the solution is not clear, and where resources are limited.[6] When an organizational crisis occurs, both good and bad can result. A crisis can lead to opportunities for learning and change[7], or of course failure for the organization. How the crisis is communicated and managed will determine whether

---

[6] Hermann, 1963; Turner, 1976; Starbuck & Hedberg, 1977; Webb, 1994.

[7] Pauchant & Mitroff, 1992

trust is preserved and even enhanced. Normally during crisis, people at the top take control over decision making, the rumor mill replaces normal communication, and people everywhere act selfishly out of concern for their own survival. In our research and consulting, however, we found leaders who have found ways to achieve the opposite: empowering everyone to solve problems, fostering open communication, and encouraging the sharing of scarce resources.

Closing a Restaurant

Dennis Quaintance recently had to close one of his restaurants, Lucky 32, in Raleigh, NC. In an open letter, this is how he communicated the closing:

Dear Guests and Staff Members of Lucky 32 on Spring Forest Road in Raleigh,

We have decided to close this wonderful restaurant. For the past 12 years it has been our great pleasure to serve this neighborhood. We will continue with our normal hours of service through brunch on Sunday, October 29th and then we will close.

The reason is simple; fewer guests are dining here. Digging around we learned that people still really like Luckys, but there are a lot more options, so our neighbors are still dining here, just less often. My bet is that a restaurant from a different category will come into this building. We considered putting in a different restaurant ourselves, but decided that our little company would be better served to focus on our hotel and restaurant under construction in Greensboro.

This certainly isn't a happy day, nor is it sad. With the shifting sands of supply and demand, healthy restaurant outfits open and close restaurants all of the time. Twelve years is a life span far beyond the norm. We are not abandoning this neck of the woods. Our restaurant in Cary is going strong. My bet is that we will bring another Lucky 32 to Raleigh in the coming years. As most of you know, we announced that we were considering our options a number of months ago. At that time, we explained to our staff that if we concluded that closing the restaurant was best, there would be bonuses for those who qualified. (FYI: Some people might choose to transfer to Cary or one of our other restaurants. This and the details of the bonuses are explained in a separate letter to our staff members.)

Thank you to those who have enjoyed dining with us and an extra special thank you to those who have been valuable members of this team.

Sincerely,

Dennis Quaintance

Dennis Quaintance

In discussing this closing, Dennis told us that the more typical scene is for employees to come to work one day at their restaurant to find it padlocked, with no advance notice or even an explanation at the door. Not only did Dennis communicate months ahead of time for the Raleigh restaurant closing, he used retention bonuses and severance payments for his employees who were going to lose their jobs, even though he said it was "unheard of in the restaurant business." He also kept a "Promise Index" which showed the consistency between the words and actions of Dennis and his management team.

Each of these actions reinforced the ROCC of Trust with these employees. According to Dennis, employees responded to these efforts in a "tremendously positive" way: no 'go to hell' emails were received from anyone. Sixteen employees transferred to his Cary, NC restaurant, even though it was 16 miles away and there were 128 restaurants in the area that they could have gone to work for instead.

One of the ways in which Dennis helps to *prevent* crises from occurring is the way in which he listens to his employees, and expects his managers to listen to them. This distinctive approach to listening is used to gauge employees' perspectives not only about the business generally, but also to learn about particularly sensitive issues or where employees might fear retribution:

We believe that if you really want to know what the staff's thinking, you've got to get them out of the (work) context. We're very careful to do this, particularly in our industry. If we think that one of our employees is troubled about work, we walk the employee to his or her car and say something like, 'Oh, where's the moon tonight?' We say something that doesn't relate to anything. That will somehow give the person permission to say, 'You know, my boss that I work with, he's coming on to me and it offends me.' We're then able to get something done before it becomes a big deal.

As our previous examples have emphasized, communicating in a humble, authentic, and courageous manner is important to building trust. As this chapter shows, communicating in such a manner is especially critical to trust during times of adversity.

Trust Tips Dos and Don'ts:

Do:

- Do establish timelines for who needs to be told what when – people need time to digest what you communicate.
- Do remember that employees want to hear from you before they read it in the *Wall Street Journal.*
- Do remember that it's impossible to over-communicate during crisis.

Don't:

- Don't shut down during times of crisis.
- Don't fail to provide your employees sufficient time to ask you questions.
- Don't forget you train your managers to be effective communicators.

In the next chapter, we describe how leaders need to remember to renew themselves in order to sustain trust with others.

IV

Taking the Next Step

22

Renew Yourself Regularly

It's good that I've pulled out. It's caused excitement, renewed energy; definitely a ripple effect through the company. - Melanie Bergeron, CEO of Two Men and a Truck, International

In order to have the strength and energy to continue to build the ROCC of Trust, it is essential that people regularly renew themselves. In our work with leaders, we found that these renewals can take many forms, but the common theme across them is that leaders removed themselves from their present circumstances and moved to situations that were quite different but still provided the opportunity for their unique talents to be used effectively. It also allowed them to step back or step away because they were able to entrust others to carry their organizations forward.

A Corporate Sabbatical

One example of providing the opportunity for renewal is the innovative human resources policy that Two Men and a Truck, International (TMT) has developed. TMT provides a six-week sabbatical for employees that have been with the firm for six years. This is not in lieu of their regularly allotted vacation time, but in *addition* to it. Prior to taking a sabbatical, an employee must cross-train colleagues on all aspects of their job so that there is no work on their desk when they return from their sabbatical. On the day that employee returns from sabbatical, they will receive an orientation about their work area and what has transpired in their absence. When this policy was initially implemented, TMT management discovered that their employees did not necessarily want to leave their jobs for 6 weeks (or did not want to stay home for 6 weeks). However, over time, it has become an important tool for the company to reenergize its employees. Through 2008, 18 employees have taken this sabbatical. As Melanie told us about their sabbatical program:

It's proved to be extremely valuable with our cross-training efforts. We're realizing that some quiet people who go on sabbatical actually have a large workload, but they haven't let us know that while they're working. Then there are other people here who we assume have a large workload, but we find out that maybe they can do more because while they're gone, other people take on their jobs with no problem at all. When our people come back from their sabbaticals, their workloads or even their entire jobs may change. That's not why we did this sabbatical program, but through our sabbaticals, we really learn about what our employees do when they're gone, and we appreciate them even more when they come back.

Jon Sorber, Executive Vice President of TMT, and a franchisee, has also instituted the sabbatical program for employees at his three franchises. As he stated, *I did a mini version of it because our turnover rate is higher than at Home Office. For my sabbatical program, I went with three years of service, three weeks off for the sabbatical. We have had about six people go through it, and they loved it. They came back rejuvenated.*

Melanie started thinking about stepping back while she went on a vacation during the summer of 2006. *"That was a wonderful experience and I dreaded coming back to the fast pace of my work – there's so much travel, and so many people you have to keep in constant contact with. The pace is draining. I started to realize quite honestly that I was getting burned out, running both the day-to-day operations as well as serving on the various external boards and participating in franchising programs.* When her brother Brig took his own sabbatical, she concluded that she needed to step back from running TMT on a daily basis and let him do it.

When Brig was gone for his sabbatical this summer, it just made me realize what a valuable person he is. I realized that I'd made Brig president but I hadn't given him any responsibility. He's always been in my shadow, being 11 months younger, but we've always been very respectful of each other. Brig was in the process of joining the Young Presidents Organization, so I asked him, 'Brig, do you want to be president?' He said, 'Yes, yes, I want full responsibility.' So I gave Brig all of my responsibilities. So Brig became President of TMT not only in title, which he received at the beginning of 2007, but in reality as well. In the summer of 2007, he acquired the title of COO as well, and has assumed full responsibility for the daily operations of TMT. As Melanie related, *"Only a month or two after I did this, he said, 'Are you sure you don't mind me taking over all the internal operations?' I said, 'no, but are you sure you want to keep doing it?' It's funny – neither of us wants to let the other person feel left out."*

Melanie has cut back her presence at the Home Office, spending more time with her family, and to focus on expanding TMT's presence in the marketplace. As Melanie concluded:

This is all so new, but it's helped me to focus on my family. I have twin 10-year-old boys and I want to actively participate in their lives. It's allowed me to pick up the boys from school. The other thing that I'm noticing is it's allowing me to get much more involved externally, as I'm working 10 to 20 hours a week at TMT. I'm very involved with the International Franchise Association (IFA); I'm chair of IFA's education committee, serve on its women's committee, and am a member of IFA's board of directors. It's very good exposure for Two Men and a Truck. It's a great learning experience and it's a good way to give back.

As Melanie's experience shows, renewing yourself can be a way to rejuvenate your organization as well.

Trust Tips Dos and Don'ts:

Do:

- Do schedule the time necessary reflect on what you're doing.
- Do find opportunities to renew yourself.
- Do develop a sabbatical program for yourself and your subordinates.

Don't:

- Don't forget to provide real breaks from work for yourself and your employees.
- Don't assume that you are using all of your talents, or that they couldn't be employed differently.
- Don't fail to develop a proper succession plan so that others can assume your position.

The next chapter considers how we as leaders might reflect on what we are doing in our organizations to discover how we can enlarge our purpose.

23

Enlarge Your Purpose

Every story, great and small, shared the same essential structure because every story we tell borrows its power from a Larger Story, a Story woven into the fabric of our being. - John Eldridge, *Epic*, p. 12.

All good leaders tell good stories, and as with all good stories, they entertain us, they inspire us, or they fire our imaginations. They also reach us emotionally, connect us to another, and thus they remind us that we are all part of something greater, as John Eldridge reminds us in his book, *Epic*. As Ted Castle told us:

I'm really interested in the relationship that a small business can have with its employees, the advantage that that provides. I try to leverage the fact that people work for

187

a small business at Rhino Foods. We're looking for people who find that to be more motivating than working at a place where they don't know the owner. The better we are at listening to our employees and knowing what their work and non-work challenges are, the better we can then provide all the opportunities to improve what we do. We try to look at the whole individual. We think that it's important to try to get people to be good at work and outside of work.

I think there's a lot to be said for stories and there's a lot to be said for people having meaning and connection. Having fun and challenging people and showing people where we are is all part of that. I believe stories are very powerful if there's a message that people can relate to it, and so we're constantly trying to find ways to engage our employees through telling stories.

It isn't really a story about me anymore. We began hiring Bosnian refugees in the late nineties, and now we have a lot of African refugees, as Burlington is an area for refugee settlement. Thirty percent of our workforce are now refugees. We look at that as a good thing for our business, bringing diversity to our business -- we think it makes us a stronger company. We are embracing this so we can get really good at integrating them.

We weren't sure how we'd be able to handle English as a second language at Rhino because we try to share so much information. We have company meetings, we have games that we play and try to turn people into stakeholders or owners. That English isn't the refugees first language caused us to ask, "how are we going do this?" As we started doing it, there were some real challenges and difficulties to it, but as we've worked through it we look at it as actually a really powerful engine for our company. We have some pretty amazing people working here. So that's an exciting story we tell about what's happening in our company now. I think that there will be a lot of stories that come out of this.

We rely on people creating an environment where people will tell us what they think, and where we're good at listening. We're not always good at it. But our fundamental belief is that we will continually rely on our employees to be a part of helping grow the company. That's how we're built. We don't look at that as taking more time or costing more money. We look at that as part of what we need to do to be good at our work.

Trust Tips Dos and Don'ts:

Do:

- Do write down your own story of how you've come to where you are today.
- Do use your stories to enlarge your purpose.
- Do encourage your employees to be part of that larger purpose.

Don't:

- Don't overlook prospective employees who may be different from you.
- Don't limit your vision of your company to your product or service.
- Don't forget to keep track of how you've achieved your goals.

In the next chapter, we explore the fact that in addition to being trustworthy, a leader must be able to trust in others.

24

Who Can You Trust?

Trust men and they will be true to you; Treat them greatly and they will show themselves great. - Ralph Waldo Emerson (Maxwell, p. 83)

While we are working to become more trustworthy to others, we also want to know who *we* can trust. As leaders, we want to surround ourselves with people who we can count on, who we can lean on as we build our business. First, who is your most reliable colleague? Is there someone you can rely on to show up for work? Who can you rely on to be consistent in the way they deal with you?

Second, who is your most open and honest colleague? It has been said that "our critics will tell us we are wrong long before our friends," but we truly value those friends and colleagues that will be open enough with us to steer us in the right direction and tell us the truth. We need to know not only how others feel about our leadership, but also about our own limitations and mistakes. As we have seen with Bob Lintz, sometimes we have to be willing to be open and honest first, in order to encourage others to be open and honest with us.

Third, who do you count on to do the job right? We might have a colleague that is honest with us, but are they also competent in the way they perform their job? Do they have the proper set of skills and abilities that enable us to trust the work that they do? Do they regularly exceed our expectations? Do they complement our own strengths and compensate for our weaknesses? Are they ambitious enough to seek further development for themselves?

Finally, who do you count on to be compassionate with you as you are caring for others? Who is that person you could call at 2 a.m. if you needed to, knowing that they would take the time to listen? Who looks out for your best interests, even when you can't identify them yourself? Who wants you to succeed and be happy, but in your own way and not in theirs? Who would you partner with in your endeavors, knowing that while they strive for their own success, they "have your back"?

The leaders we have identified here are trustworthy in all four dimensions: they are reliable, open and honest, competent, and compassionate. In addition, their courage, authenticity and humility enable them to trust their subordinates and colleagues to bring out the best in them.

Many people have fallen prey either to trusting the wrong people or not trusting anybody. Those leaders who have trusted others have not only empowered them, but have enabled their organizations to thrive as well, by harnessing the power of people who trust one another.

In diagnosing the level of trust in organizations and within teams, we use the following survey questions. We have used this survey with leaders in scores of many different organizations. The questions can be used to assess how much individuals believe their managers or leaders to be trustworthy. It can also be helpful to figure out which pieces of the ROCC are strong and those which need to be further developed. Feel free to use these questions to assess the level of trust that exists in your organization.

Trust Scale (using a 1-5 scale)

This person is straightforward with me..............................

This person is competent and knowledgeable...................

This person does not try to get out of his/her commitments...

This person does not take advantage of me......................

This person communicates honestly with me...................

This person can contribute to my organization's success...

This person behaves consistently......................................

This person does not exploit me...

This person does not mislead me in his/her communications ....

This person can help my organization survive during the next decade ....

This person is reliable ....

This person cares about my best interests ....

This person does not withhold important information from me..

This person is concerned for my welfare ....

This person can be counted on ....

This person can help solve important problems faced by my organization ....

Trust Tips Dos and Don'ts:

Do:

- Do find someone to be a proofreader (Reliability).
- Do learn who is willing to tell you the truth (Openness).
- Do find someone who you can count on to exceed your expectations. (Competence).
- Do learn who you can trust to rejuvenate you. (Compassion).

Don't:

- Don't assume that each person is equally capable in refining your ROCC of Trust – some may be better at refining certain pieces over others.
- Don't assume that no one can be trusted.
- Don't fail to give opportunities for others to demonstrate their trustworthiness.

Finally we need to know where to start to build trust with others. This last chapter provides some guidance on how to proceed.

25

Where will you start?

You can't build a reputation on what you're going to do. - Henry Ford (Maxwell, p. 50)

We have identified the importance of all four pieces of the ROCC of Trust, and realize that we all come to the party with different talents and abilities. For example, some of us are by nature very honest and open, while others prefer to keep to themselves. We need to understand ourselves well enough to recognize which of the four dimensions we are best at so that we can start there. If you feel like you are competent at your job, then start finding ways to reinforce that you are a reliable leader as well. Do one thing at a time to build your strengths by engaging in each of the four dimensions one at a time until you are as solid as a ROCC.

Individual Trust

If you don't know where to start, think about what you are best at and start there. For each piece of the ROCC of Trust, determine the level where you can currently perform. Are you performing at a minimum, moderate, or high level? Once you've completed this self-assessment, then ask others you trust where they think you operate. Finally, once you've identified which level you are at, find ways to push yourself to the next level.

THE ROCC OF TRUST

Reliability

Minimum: Inform others when you can't keep your commitments.

Moderate: Do what you say you will do.

High: Deliver upon your promises early.

Openness

Minimum: Do not lie to others.

Moderate: Tell people what they need to know.

High: Tell people the whole truth, even if it hurts you.

Competence

Minimum: Fix your mistakes.

Moderate: Do your job.

High: Exceed others' expectations.

Compassion

Minimum: Don't take advantage of someone else.

Moderate: Identify common interests and find ways to support them.

High: Help others even if it means subordinating your own interests.

Mutual Trust

Another focus of building trust is by building mutual trust with another person. There are times we are entering into a new working relationship with someone and we want to believe we can trust them, so we enter into a working relationship without a legal contract. One alternative to a legal contract is this *ROCC Star Pledge* in which each person promises to act trustworthy.

The ROCC Star Pledge

1. We promise to be reliable in our work together. We promise to tell each other if there are problems that will keep us from meeting our agreed upon deadlines.
2. We promise to be open and honest with each other. We agree to tell the truth about our work together.
3. We promise to do our best work for each other. We plan to exceed each others' expectations.
4. We promise to care about each others interests and to promote each others well-being.

We are ROCC Stars

Me _____   You _____

Building the ROCC of Trust begins by being an authentic person—in your own way. No two people will build the ROCC of Trust the same way. The leaders we have profiled in this book built the ROCC of Trust with their various stakeholders in a wide variety of ways, but each in his or her own unique approach. We encourage you to embrace your own unique combination of talents, skills and experience as you work to become a more courageous, authentic and humble leader. Please share your own stories with us as you work to build the ROCC of Trust with others. We look forward to hearing from you.

Aneil and Karen Mishra

trustdr@gmail.com

www.totaltrust.wordpress.com

Appendix A

Biographies of the individuals profiled in this book

Kay Ashburn, RN

Wake Forest University Baptist Medical Center

Throughout life, I have had several aspirations. Perhaps the greatest of these is the desire to help people through either the resources of medicine or merely by the means of being a compassionate, trustworthy and honest friend. Having achieved my primary goal of being a registered nurse, I have devoted much of my life to the children and adults that I help. Not only that, but I have also become part of their "beacon of hope" in the world of cystic fibrosis and other pulmonary diseases. These patients trust me -- something that I have always longed for. Through relationships based on trust, I adamantly believe that one can accomplish his or her greatest aspirations such as I have at Wake Forest University Baptist Medical Center.

Melanie Bergeron,

CEO, TWO MEN AND A TRUCK®/INTERNATIONAL, INC.

Melanie Bergeron officially joined the family business in 1989 when she was awarded the first TWO MEN AND A TRUCK® franchise in Atlanta, Ga. Bergeron also maintained a career in pharmaceutical sales while operating the franchise because she reinvested all of her profits back into the franchise. Eventually she left her pharmaceutical sales career to focus on her franchise full-time. At the request of her mother, Founder and CEO Mary Ellen Sheets, Bergeron came to work at the home office in Lansing, Michigan in the 1990s. In 1994, Bergeron was named president of TWO MEN AND A TRUCK®. In 2002, she became chief operating officer and in January 2007, she took over as CEO.

Together with her mother and her two brothers, Melanie has incorporated a vision, a positive team atmosphere, ongoing support, compassion and commitment in the working environment at TWO MEN AND A TRUCK®. She is a graduate of Central Michigan University in Mt. Pleasant, Mich. with a bachelor's degree in marketing and business administration, and she achieved the Certified Franchise Executive certification, a recognized standard of excellence in the franchise industry.

Melanie is a Member of the Young Presidents Association, is active on the Board of Governors for the Institute of Certified Franchise Executives , is a member of the board of directors for the certification board of the International Franchise Association (ICFE), and is a member of Central Michigan University Dean's Business Advisory Council.

Ted Castle

President and Founder, Rhino Foods

A native of Rochester, New York, Ted has known success in many arenas. The arena is an appropriate metaphor, for Castle first discovered his leadership skills on the athletic fields, specifically as an All American and captain of the University of Vermont's hockey team. Upon graduation in 1974, and after leading his team to a championship season, Castle moved into the world of professional sports, where he played hockey on the European continent for two seasons. Sports continued to be fertile ground for Castle, and on his return from

Europe, he took assistant hockey coaching jobs, first at the University of Maine and then later at his alma mater.

In 1986, Castle traded in his coaching garb to devote full-time energy to his small business, and soon after that Rhino Foods began to work with Ben and Jerry's Homemade of Waterbury, Vermont. These efforts culminated in the nationwide release in spring of 1991 of Chocolate Chip Cookie Dough Ice Cream. Today, Ted Castle runs a company of some 140 employees, manufacturing a variety of frozen desserts and ice cream products that are distributed in North America under proprietary Rhino names, as well as through private label agreements with major food marketers and supermarket chains. Rhino Foods manufactures cheesecake, ice cream cookie sandwiches, bakery products and inclusions for ice cream manufacturers. Rhino's customer list includes national accounts such as Ben & Jerry's, Hood, Friendly's, Weight Watchers and Nestlé USA.

Castle's success has not gone unnoticed and both he and his company have garnered their share of awards. Castle was selected as *Vermont Small Business Person of the Year* by the United States Small Business Administration, and a regional award winner in Ernst & Young's and *Inc.* magazine's Entrepreneur of the Year Award. Rhino Foods has been awarded with the US

Chamber of Commerce *Blue Chip Enterprise Award* from Child Help USA for its efforts on behalf of Vermont children and families, and received the Optimas award for vision in the workplace (past winners include UPS, Coors and 3M), *Inc.* magazine's Best Companies to Work For, United Way Cornerstone Award, and State of VT *Climate Wise Award.* Ted has served on the Board of Directors for Prevent Child Abuse Vermont, United Way of Vermont and Shelburne Farms. Ted was honored as the *Outstanding Alumnus* by the University of Vermont's College of Agriculture and Life Sciences in 1997.

Ted makes time to enjoy the quality of life that Vermont offers. He is an avid water skier and sailboat enthusiast, and when winter arrives he skies and breaks out his old hockey skates for pickup games on the family pond. Castle shares his country home with his wife Anne, and two sons Ned and Rooney.

Barbara Esterly, RN

Department of Otolaryngology/Head and Neck Surgery
University of North Carolina at Chapel Hill

Barbara is a wife, a mother of two lovely daughters, and a grandmother to six beautiful grandchildren who call her Nanny. Originally from Maine, she graduated from the Mary Fletcher Hospital School of Nursing in

Burlington, VT. After several years in Maine her husband's job relocated them to the south and ultimately brought them to Chapel Hill, NC. She has worked in the UNC ENT clinic seven years and loves it. She feels very fortunate to be able to work along side such a dedicated and caring group of professionals. She still roots for the Boston Red Sox and New England Patriots; however, she does not miss the long and harsh winters of New England. She loves to knit and sew, but her greatest hobby is her grandchildren.

Alan Finkel, MD

Professor and Director, University Headache Clinic

Department of Neurology at the University of North Carolina

Dr. Finkel earned his B.A. degree in English from Middlebury College in 1975, and his MD from School of Medicine at SUNY at Buffalo in 1985 where he did his honors thesis in neuroanatomy. He completed post-graduate medical education internal medicine at the University of Alabama-Birmingham, and neurology at the University of North Carolina-Chapel Hill. He also completed a fellowship in pain management and headache medicine in the Department of Neurology at the University of North Carolina, Chapel Hill, North Carolina.

He has published over a dozen refereed journal articles and numerous book chapters on headache and facial pain. He serves or has served on the editorial boards of *Headache; Neurology; Cephalalgia; Lancet- Neurology; and Neuropsychopharmacology.*

Dr. Finkel is the recipient of several honors and awards including the John R Graham Senior Clinicians' Forum Award, from American Headache Society (2006), the Teaching Excellence Award from the UNC School of Medicine (2005), and the Teacher Recognition Award from American Academy of Neurology (2006). He serves as Chair of the Headache and Face Pain Section of the American Academy of Neurology (AAN), is a board member of the United Council of Neurologic Subspecialties (UCNS), and is a Fellow of the American Headache Society (AHS).

Karen Fisher, RN

University of North Carolina at Chapel Hill Department of Neurology

In Chicago, on a Christmas morn
To first-generation Polish-Americans born.

Married the high school sweetheart as intended

Two boys, one girl, love extended.

Back to school wearing hat in white
learning skills to heal with all my might.

Caring for the great and small
with headache pain overall.

Side by side with Dr. Finkel
our busy days shine and twinkle.

Approaching each day with orange-colored glasses
Savoring each moment as it passes.

Bob Lintz

Retired Plant Manager, General Motors

Member of the Board of Trustees, The Cleveland Clinic

A native of Flint, Michigan, Bob Lintz received his Bachelor's degree in Industrial Management from Michigan State University in East Lansing, Michigan in 1962. He also attended the Management Excellence Program at Case Western University's Weatherhead School of Management. Bob began his General Motors career right after college as a College Graduate-in-Training at the Flint Metal Fabricating Plant. After serving in various positions there, he was named Superintendent of Inspection and Quality Control at the GM Bay City, Michigan Plant in 1972. In September 1974, he was transferred to the GM Parma Pressed Metal Plant as General Superintendent Manufacturing and on September 1, 1980, he was promoted to Plant Manager of the Pressed Metal operation. In February of 1987, he became Manager of the entire Parma Complex. He retired from General Motors in 2004.

Throughout his adult life, Bob has been very active in community affairs. Among his many current philanthropic and service activities, Bob is a member of the Board of Trustees of the Cleveland Clinic, where he serves on the marketing, research, education, and audit committees. He is also a member of the Board of Trustees for the Cleveland Clinic's Western Region hospitals where he is also a member of the governance committee. Finally, he has been active for many years with the Boys Hope/Girls Hope Foundation, where he is currently a member of the golf tournament committee. He also owns the original vehicle from the *Ghostbusters* movie, which he fully restored and which contains the four original "proton packs" worn by the Ghostbusters. Bob uses this vehicle to raise money for many local charities.

Kevin Lobdell, MD

Director of the Adult and Pediatric CV Critical Care and Associate Director of the Cardiothoracic Residency Program

Carolinas Heart and Vascular Institute in Charlotte, North Carolina

Dr. Lobdell is from Detroit, MI. He graduated from the University of Michigan and Wayne State University School of Medicine, and his general surgery training was at the University of Minnesota. He was the Winchester Fellow in cardiothoracic surgery research at Yale University, where he completed his residency in cardiothoracic surgery. While at the Children's Hospital of Philadelphia and Royal Children's Hospital in Melbourne, Australia, Dr. Lobdell completed congenital cardiac surgery fellowships (working with Drs. Jacobs, Spray, and Karl). His surgical critical care training was at the Children's Hospital of Michigan/Wayne State University. Dr. Lobdell has extensive experience in both pediatric and adult cardiothoracic surgery. He is certified by the American Board of Surgery and the American Board of Thoracic Surgery and has special qualification and surgical critical care by the American Board of Surgery.

His research interests include clinical process improvement, systems engineering and safety, group interactions in high risk environments, and sedation monitoring. His clinical interests include quality management, value-based competition, data analysis, neonatal heart surgery, and cardiac critical care.

Dennis W. Quaintance

CEO, Quaintance-Weaver Restaurants & Hotels

Dennis' spirit of entrepreneurship started at age eight when we scoured the desert for interesting sedimentary rocks, polish them, and sold them as "wonder stones" along a desolate stretch of a Nevada highway. He began his hospitality career at age 15 as a housekeeper's assistant at a hotel in Missoula, Montana. He quickly worked his way up to assistant general manager. For four years after high school, we worked in leadership at several hotels around the Northwest. In 1979, he moved to Greensboro, North Carolina, to open a new restaurant, Franklin's Off Friendly. In 1988, Dennis teamed up with Mike Weaver to form Quaintance-Weaver and opened Lucky 32 restaurant in Greensboro in 1989. Today, the family of Quaintance-Weaver Restaurants and Hotels includes Lucky 32 Kitchen and Wine Bar in Greensboro and Cary (2001) and four additional businesses within a mile of the original Lucky 32: the 131-room O.Henry Hotel (1998); the Green Valley Grill (1998); the 147-room

Proximity Hotel (2007); and Print Works Bistro (2007). Recipient of the Junior Achievement of the Triad "Spirit of Entrepreneurship" Award in 2006, Dennis currently serves as Executive in Residence for the Center for Creative Leadership and a board member for the Johnnetta B. Cole Global Institute for Diversity and Inclusion. He and his wife, Nancy King Quaintance, have twin children, Kathleen Troy and Dennis Carlisle.

Bruce K. Rubin, MD
Professor and Vice Chair of Pediatrics
Professor of Physiology and Pharmacology, and Professor of Biomedical Engineering
Wake Forest University School of Medicine
Co-Medical Director of Respiratory Care at Baptist Hospital

Dr. Rubin earned his BSc, Master of Engineering, and MD degrees from Tulane University in New Orleans. After completing medical studies, Dr. Rubin went to Oxford University as a Rhodes Scholar to do postdoctoral work in biomedical engineering. In 1983 Dr. Rubin joined the faculty of Queen's University in Kingston, Ontario as Chief of Pediatric Respirology and Critical Care. From 1987-91 he was a scientist at the University of Alberta. From 1991-97 he was Professor of Pediatrics and Chief of

Pediatric Pulmonary at St. Louis University. Since 1997 Dr. Rubin has been at the Wake Forest University School of Medicine in Winston-Salem. He completed an MBA at the Babcock School of Management, Wake Forest University in 2004.

Dr. Rubin's research is regulation of mucus clearance in health and disease and aerosol delivery of medications. He directs the only comprehensive Mucus Clearance Disorder's clinic in the United States for the assessment and treatment of adults and children with difficulty to manage mucus problems. Dr. Rubin' group has focused on studying the relationship between secretion properties and clearance, aerosol therapy, and adherence to prescribed therapy in persons with chronic lung disease. The goal of this research group is to develop new therapies for asthma, cystic fibrosis, and chronic bronchitis.

Dr. Rubin is on the editorial boards of 12 pulmonary journals and is an associate editor for six of these. He is also the specialty director for Pediatric Pulmonary of the Academy of Sciences *Faculty of 1000*. He has published more than 200 research papers and chapters and holds five patents. His latest books, *Therapy for Mucus Clearance Disorders* and *Immunomodulation by Antibiotics* were both published in 2004.

Dr. Rubin received the ACCP Young Investigator award in 1989, the Critical Care Research Award in 1990, the Alfred Soffer Award for Editorial Excellence in 2004, and the Career Achievement Award from the American Association for Respiratory Care in 2007. He is listed in *Who's Who in Science and Engineering, Who's Who in the United States*, and *The Best Doctors in America*. He is a Fellow of the Royal College of Physicians in Canada, the American College of Chest Physicians, and a member of the American Pediatric Association. Dr. Rubin is also a Fellow of the American Association for Respiratory Care and a Trustee of the American Respiratory Care Foundation.

Brent Senior, MD

Associate Professor of Otolaryngology/Head and Neck Surgery and

Chief of Rhinology, Allergy, and Sinus Surgery at the University of North Carolina at Chapel Hill.

Brent A. Senior, MD, FACS, FARS graduated from the Wheaton College in Wheaton, Illinois in 1986 and received his medical degree from the University of Michigan in 1990. His internship in General Surgery was completed at Boston University in 1991, followed by a residency in otolaryngology/head and neck surgery at the combined

216

otolaryngology residency training program at Tufts University and Boston University. In 1996, he completed a fellowship in rhinology and sinus surgery at the University of Pennsylvania under Dr. David Kennedy. He joined the Department of Otolaryngology/Head and Neck Surgery at Henry Ford Hospital as a Senior Staff Surgeon in 1996, leaving to join the faculty of the University of North Carolina in 1999. He currently serves as Associate Professor of Otolaryngology/Head and Neck Surgery and Chief of Rhinology, Allergy, and Sinus Surgery at the University of North Carolina at Chapel Hill.

Dr. Senior serves on the editorial boards of the *American Journal of Rhinology*, *Laryngoscope*, and *Rhinology* and he is formerly an Associate Editor of *Otolaryngology/Head and Neck Surgery*. He currently serves the American Board of Otolaryngology as a Senior Examiner, and the AAO/HNS Foundation as a member of the Rhinology and Paranasal Sinuses Committee and the Humanitarian Efforts Committee. He also currently serves as Secretary/Treasurer for the Christian Society of Otolaryngology/Head and Neck Surgeons and as Secretary and Second Vice President of the American Rhinologic Society.

Having a passion for education, Dr. Senior has received numerous awards and honors including teacher of the

217

year, Best Doctors in North Carolina, and Best Doctors in the USA. He has received the *Honor* award from the American Academy of Otolaryngology/Head and Neck Surgery and has served as Director and/or instructor in sinus surgery and rhinology in over 60 national and international courses. He has published over 70 articles and book chapters and edited a book on sinus surgery. Having a great interest in mission work and education in developing countries, Dr. Senior has participated and organized 10 trips to Vietnam focusing on otolaryngology education. In 2005, he received the *Humanitarian Award* from the American Academy of Otolaryngology/Head and Neck Surgery and the *Medal of Honor* from Ho Chi Minh City in Vietnam for service to its people. In 2007, he received a medal and citation from the Minister of Health of Vietnam for his service to the people of Vietnam.

Mary Ellen Sheets

Founder, TWO MEN AND A TRUCK®/INTERNATIONAL, Inc.

In less than 20 years, Mary Ellen Sheets has taken her sons' small moving business and driven it to an international corporation with more than 1,300 trucks and more than 200 locations worldwide. After her sons, Brig and Jon Sorber, left for college, the business continued to receive numerous requests so Sheets decided to take it over. She purchased an old moving truck for $350 – the only money she ever invested in the company – and hired two movers. The business grew steadily and Sheets' entrepreneurial spirit became well known in the Lansing area. Eventually, she quit her state government job (foregoing her retirement) to put 100 percent into her thriving moving business. She awarded the first franchise to her daughter, Melanie Bergeron, a year later. It was located in Atlanta, Ga. By 1989, Sheets had developed the business into the first and only local moving franchise in the country. In 2007, TWO MEN AND A TRUCK®/INTERNATIONAL, Inc.'s annual revenue was $200 million dollars.

Sheets considers herself fortunate to have her daughter, Melanie Bergeron, and sons Brig and Jon Sorber, the original "two men," playing active roles in the company. "When I look back, I can't believe this all happened," she says. "I am in shock and so grateful. I definitely think this is the American dream. We live in a wonderful country."

Mary Ellen has received numerous awards. In 2004, she was named the Entrepreneur of the Year by the International Franchise Association for her vision and savvy. She was the first woman to earn this award in its

40 year history. She has also been honored as the: 2004 *Michigan Women's Foundation Women of Achievement and Courage* Award, 2002 *Athena Award*, 1999 *Working Women's 500 Congress*, 1999 *Working Women's Best Employer Regional Finalist*, 1998 *Blue Chip Award*, 1995 *Michigan Entrepreneur of the Year Award*, 1994 Top 25 *Michigan Business Woman of the Year*, and the 1993 *Lansing Chamber of Commerce Small Business Person of the Year*.

A key portion of Sheets' business model is to give back to the community. Always active in local service projects, TWO MEN AND A TRUCK®'s commitment to the community began with Sheets. At the end of her first year in business, she profited $1,000 and then donated all of it -- giving $100 to 10 different charities. Sheets is a long-time supporter of many organizations including: Habitat for Humanity; the United Way of America; the YMCA; the Greater Lansing Food Bank; the Potter Park Zoo; the Michigan Vietnam Monument Organization; and the American Cancer Society.

Reverend Jean Smith

Retired Executive Director, Seamen's Church Institute of New York and New Jersey

The Rev. Dr. Jean Smith was Executive Director of the Seamen's Church Institute of New York & New Jersey (SCI) and was responsible for the largest independent maritime-oriented non-profit in North America whose 2007 budget was over $7.5 million. Founded in 1834, SCI is an ecumenical agency affiliated wit the Episcopal Diocese of New York.

The Seamen's Church Institute includes the Center for Seafarers' Services, which provides pastoral care for the personnel of 3,400 vessels annually in the Port of New York & New Jersey. SCI also operates the Center for Maritime Education which trains nearly 1,600 mariners each year through its simulator-based training centers in New York, Kentucky, and Texas; and the Center for Seafarer's Rights, which is internationally renowned for its legal advocacy work,

Jean Smith, a native of Missouri, graduated from Northwester University in Evanston Illinois, with a B.S in speech therapy. She married Peter Smith whose international business career took them abroad. Peter, jean their two small children lived six years in Paris and Tokyo.

When the family returned to the United States, Jean was drawn closer to her Episcopal faith. After graduating with a Masters of Divinity in 1980 from the Church

Divinity School of the Pacific (CDSP) in Berkeley, California, she was ordained by Bishop G.P. Mellick Belshaw of New Jersey. In 1998, CDSP awarded her an honorary doctorate.

Her parish work took her to Trinity Church in Princeton, New Jersey, where she eventually served as Interim Rector. At Trinity, she led a clergy staff of seven and a lay staff of 12 along with dozens of volunteer individuals and committees who served the parish to fulfill its missions.

Jean left Trinity in 1990 to become the Director of SCI's International Seafarers' Center in Port Newark. She was in charge of operating a center with a multi-million dollar budget and supervising chaplains and ship visitors. She initiated a ministry to truckers, and an annual Port Community Festival to enhance community spirit to this large intermodal port.

In 1995, Jean became the Seamen's Church Institute's Managing Director and Chief Operating Officer. In 1998, the Center for Maritime Education created training for inland mariners, and Jean developed a pastoral and business plan for Ministry on the River. No other agency or denomination had ever been successful in a large-scale ecumenical, pastoral program to inland mariners. Seamen's Church Institute's "Ministry on the River" program is now the only network of pastoral care available to more than 30,000 inland mariners along America's 2,200 miles of inland waterways. Chaplains not only bless boats and visit with mariners onboard, but also respond to calls made to SCI's free 1-800 pastoral emergency number. As inland ministry gained momentum, so did the Institute's international training program for port chaplains. The Asian/North American Pastoral Training Center program that she took over in 1990 was transformed into the International Training Center for Workplace Ministry (ITC).

Jean became SCI's Executive Director in 2002, only the eighth Executive Director in SCI's history. Interns from around the world came to the Center for SCI Training. Jean then used her teaching background that included experience both in the United States and overseas to hone the ITC curriculum until it struck the right balance of action, reflection, and achievement. Jean retired at the end of 2007, receiving from SCI its *Lifetime Achievement Award*. She and her husband Peter now reside in Vermont. They have two grown children, Lindsay and Davis, and four grandchildren.

Brig Sorber
President and Chief Operating Officer

TWO MEN AND A TRUCK®/INTERNATIONAL, INC.

Brig Sorber is one of the original two men along with younger brother Jon Sorber. The two started the business in the early 1980s in Okemos, Mich. to earn spending money. Using a 1967 pickup truck, the brothers placed an ad in a local shopping guide that read "Men At Work Movers...Two Men and A Truck." The ad also included a stick figure logo designed by their mother, Mary Ellen Sheets. This logo remains the corporate symbol for the now TWO MEN AND A TRUCK®/INTERNATIONAL, Inc.

After he left home to attend Northern Michigan University, Sheets decided to keep the business rolling. Upon graduation, Sorber worked as an insurance agent in Michigan's upper peninsula. He also operated his own TWO MEN AND A TRUCK® franchise in Marquette with his wife Francine. In September 1996, the Sorbers sold their franchise to come home to Lansing so they could help Sheets and sister, CEO Melanie Bergeron, restructure the TWO MEN AND A TRUCK® system. Sorber then served as a field consultant and was also in charge of franchise recruitment. As of January 2007, Brig assumed the role of president.

Brig is a graduate of Northern Michigan University with a degree in geography and an emphasis on urban planning and land use regulation. He is also a Certified

Franchise Executive (a recognized standard of excellence in the franchise industry). Brig feels that his experience as a mover, driver and a franchisee helps him to make well-educated decisions that benefit the TWO MEN AND A TRUCK® system as a whole.

Brig has been inducted into the Minorities in Franchising committee of the International Franchise Association. This committee aims to increase the number and success of minorities in franchising. He has also been past president of Okemos Baseball Softball Club, and is a member of Knights of Columbus.

Jon Sorber

Executive Vice President

TWO MEN AND A TRUCK® /INTERNATIONAL, Inc.

Franchisee, Two Men and a Truck Lansing and Grand Rapids

Jon Sorber is one of the original two men along with older brother Brig Sorber. Jon opened his first franchise in Grand Rapids in 1989. He worked at his childhood desk, behind the couch in his one-bedroom apartment that also served as his office. His customer service representative also worked from home. At that time, Sorber was only earning about $50 a week. He had to take a job with UPS to subsidize his income. He worked at

UPS from 4 a.m. to 8 a.m. and then focused on his TWO MEN AND A TRUCK® franchise from 8 a.m. to 5 p.m. Sorber often did additional paperwork at night. In 1990, he quit his job in corporate security in Grand Rapids to focus on the family business. Today, Sorber has more than 150 employees at his three locations.

Besides running his three franchises, Sorber plays a role on the company's board of directors. As the only board member actively running franchises, Sorber frequently test markets new services, products and systems. Wearing two hats, one as franchisee and the other as franchisor, he also works as a "sounding board" between the franchisees and the franchisor. He is a graduate of Northern Michigan University in Marquette, Mich. with a bachelor's degree in criminal justice.

Jon has been awarded the Friends of West Michigan Business Grand Rapids Chamber of Commerce award, and in 2004, the Political Action Committee 9th Annual Salute Award. He serves as a board member of the Greater Lansing Home Builders Association. He is also a member of the Greater Grand Rapids Home Builders Association, the Grand Rapids Association of Realtors, the Lansing Regional Chamber of Commerce, the St. Johns Chamber of Commerce, the Greater Grand Rapids Chamber of Commerce, the Wyoming Chamber of

Commerce, and the Barry County Chamber of Commerce. He is also very actively involved as a member of the Brightside Community Church in Caledonia, Michigan.

Appendix B

Our Published Research Validating the ROCC of Trust

Brockner, Joel, Spreitzer, Gretchen M., Mishra, Aneil, K., Hochwarter, Wayne, Pepper, Lewis, & Weinberg, Janice. (2004) Perceived Control as an Antidote to the Negative Effects of Layoffs on Survivors' Organizational Commitment and Job Performance, Administrative Science Quarterly, 49 (1/March): 76-100.

Spreitzer, Gretchen M. and Mishra, Aneil K. (2002) To stay or to go: Voluntary survivor turnover following a downsizing, Journal of Organizational Behavior, 23, (September): 707-729.

Spreitzer, Gretchen. M. and Mishra, Aneil K. (1999) Giving Up Control Without Losing Control: Trust and Its Substitutes' Effects on Managers' Involving Employees in Decision Making. Group and Organization Management, 14 (2): 155-187.

Mishra, Aneil K and Spreitzer, Gretchen M. (1998) Explaining How Survivors Respond to Downsizing: The Roles of Trust, Empowerment, Justice and Work Redesign. Academy of Management Review, 23 (3): 567-588.

Mishra, Karen E., Spreitzer, Gretchen M., and Mishra, Aneil K. (1998) Preserving employee morale during downsizing, Sloan Management Review, 39 (2): 83-95.

Mishra, Aneil K. and Mishra, Karen E. (1994) The role of mutual trust in effective downsizing strategies, Human Resource Management, 33 (2), 261-279.

Spreitzer, Gretchen M., Noble, Deborah S., Mishra, Aneil K., & Cooke, William N. (1999) Predicting process improvement team performance in an automotive firm: Explicating the roles of trust and empowerment. In Beta Mannix, Ruth Wageman, and Margaret Neale (Eds.), Research on Managing in Groups and Teams, 2, 71-92. Stamford, CT: JAI Press

Mishra, Aneil K. (1996) Organizational responses to
crisis: The centrality of trust. In Roderick Kramer
& Thomas Tyler (Eds.). <u>Trust in Organizations:
Frontiers of theory and research</u>, 261-287.
Thousand Oaks, CA: Sage.

Index

25, 31, 33, 37, 39, 40,
44, 45, 46, 55, 65, 81,
90, 100, 102, 104, 114,
120, 121, 124, 127,
139, 140, 163, 165,
176, 181, 195, 197,
198, 201, 229

Trust Tips, 11, 12, 14,
23, 31, 37, 44, 54, 63,
70, 77, 82, 88, 95, 111,

115, 124, 137, 143,
151, 161, 171, 178,
186, 190, 195

Two Men and a Truck,
16, 29, 80, 81, 118,
153, 181, 182, 185,
204, 218, 219, 220,
224, 225, 226, 238,
240

Designated Charitable Organizations

As a way to thank the leaders we have profiled, we will be donating a portion of the proceeds from the sale of this book to following charities selected by these leaders:

American Cancer Society

The Cleveland Clinic Foundation

The Johnnetta B. Cole Global Diversity & Inclusion Institute at Bennett College for Women

REI-Vietnam based in Colorado Springs

The Seamen's Church Institute of New York and New Jersey

The University of North Carolina at Chapel Hill School of Medicine

Wake Forest University School of Medicine

Authors' Biographies

Aneil K. Mishra

Aneil will be joining the faculty of Michigan State University in the summer of 2009 where he will be Professor and Director of Executive Education for the School of Labor and Industrial Relations. He received his A.B., *cum laude*, in Economics from Princeton University in 1984, and his Ph.D. in Business Administration from the University of Michigan in 1992.

Prior to joining the faculty of MSU, Aneil was Visiting Associate Professor of Management at Duke University's Fuqua School of Business from 2008 through 2009. He previously served on the business school faculties of Wake Forest University (earning tenure there in 2001), The Pennsylvania State University and Michigan State University. Aneil's teaching and research interests include the dynamics of trust within and across organizations, leading effective organizational change and organizational culture. He has consulted for and conducted research on these issues with a number of *Fortune 500* and other firms, including AlliedSignal, Kodak, Deutsche Bank, General Motors, SC Johnson, and Two Men and a Truck. Aneil currently teaches in several executive programs at the University of Michigan Ross School of Business, including Turkey and South America. He is an executive coach at Duke University and conducts custom executive education programs. Prior to obtaining his Ph.D., Aneil worked for the General Motors Corporation as a human resource specialist and manufacturing engineer. Aneil is a member of the Academy of Management, and served on the board of directors of Cancer Services, Inc, a not-for-profit based in Winston-Salem, NC.

Aneil's research has appeared in a number of scholarly and practitioner journals including the *Academy of Management Review, Administrative Science Quarterly, Sloan Management Review, Organization Science, Human Resource Management, Journal of Organizational Behavior, Industrial and Labor Relations Review, Group & Organization Management, the Academy of Management Executive, Medical Care Research and Review, and The Milbank Quarterly,* and has been cited over 850 times in peer-reviewed journals. He currently serves on the editorial boards of the *Journal of Organizational Behavior* and the *Journal of Applied Behavioral Science*, and served as a past editorial board member of *Decision Sciences Journal of Innovative Education* from 2001-2005. He earned Wake Forest University's *Babcock Educator of the Year Award* twice, from the 2008 and 2007 Charlotte Saturday MBA students, and also earned teaching awards at both Michigan State University and Penn State University.

Karen E. Mishra

Karen will be joining the faculty of Michigan State University in the fall of 2009 where she will be Assistant Professor in the Department of Advertising, Public Relations, and Retailing in the School of Communication Arts and Sciences. She previously was an Assistant Professor in the School of Business at Meredith College in Raleigh, NC where she taught marketing and advertising from 2007 through 2009. She earned her B.A. in a dual major in Economics and Music from Albion College in 1985. In 1988, she earned her M.B.A. from the University of Michigan where she was President of the Student Council. In 2007, Karen earned her Ph.D. in

Marketing Communication from the University of North Carolina at Chapel Hill.

She previously taught marketing at Wake Forest University and The Pennsylvania State University. Karen's research interest focuses on how organizations build trust with employees through internal communication. She has consulted for a variety of organizations in the areas of marketing, sales, and customer service, including Deutsche Bank, SC Johnson, and Two Men and a Truck. Karen has conducted executive coaching at Duke University's Fuqua School of Business, and has developed and delivered custom executive education programs for a variety of for-profit and not-for-profit organizations.

Prior to obtaining her Ph.D., Karen worked for General Motors as a Human Resources Recruiter and at Johnson Controls where she managed the $75 million Pepsi-Cola account. She has served as board president of Samaritan Ministries, a not-for-profit based in Winston-Salem, NC and has served on the boards of the ARC and Leadership Winston-Salem.

Karen has published her research in *Sloan Management Review, Human Resource Management, Public Relations Review, Marketing News, and the Journal of Relationship Marketing.*